GET A YES!

The Fundamentals of
Answered Prayer

DR. F. ALLAN OLORUNSOLA

Foreword by Rev. George Adegboye

PRAISE FOR GET A YES!

Exhaustive study and a concise presentation on a particularly important subject, Pastor Allan Olorunsola unpacked crucial knowledge needs on prayer and answers, plus very important notes on the crucial knowledge needs.

- Apostle Daniel Olufemi
Kings Dominion Christian Center. Sagamu, Nigeria

The psalmist, David, reveals in Psalm 103:7 that "God made known his WAYS unto Moses, His ACTS unto the children of Israel." Prayer is not just a science but more than an ART. Dr. Allan Olorunsola in this book "Get A Yes!," has painstakingly laid out for us here to know the acceptable WAYS of God in carrying out the ART of praying to genuinely experience the ACTS of God by pouring in and on us cool water to quench the burning desire in our hearts, giving us the 'The Yes' we long for before we set out to pray. These WAYS will lead to the ART and the art to manifest the ACTS. If you're sincerely hunting for a good material to set your prayer life ablaze, through the power of the Holy Ghost and fire, grasp this piece and you'll watch you burning in your 'closet,' and you'll definitely begin to see outstanding changes in your situations and circumstances in record time, through our Lord Jesus Christ.

- Dr. Israel Joseph
The Blessing Mandate: Inspirational Branding System Coach.
Lagos, Nigeria.

"Get a YES!" is a refreshing and practical version on the topic of prayer. The title appeals to positivity and hope, inspiring the reader to dive into the contents of the book. This book contains a vivid description of the fundamental principles of Jesus' recommended pattern of prayer dotted with personal testimonies. For anyone who has asked, "Does prayer really work?" this book takes one into the What, the Why, and the How of prayer as a "supernatural force" in earthly matters.

- Ms. Olumide Osunyomi
Financial Coach, Trainer, and Speaker

"The understanding of prayer has changed for many over the years. What was once deemed necessary, always, and sacred has become a cumbersome and tedious exercise for many. when prayer is called just as an answer to an undesirable event - looking for a bailout from trouble and not a relationship - a desire to commune and hear the voice of our father and mentor, it loses its importance and appeal. In this book, prepare to learn the true essence of prayer all over again, the reason why we pray and must pray, the responsibility we must own in being specific when we talk to our heavenly father in prayer, and the peace we must learn when we receive or don't receive that which we asked for.

- D'EVA (Ebony "Ade" Bankole-Laoye)
Host, Solemn Assembly and Author "Dairy of the Called.

Someone has rightly said that prayer is the least understood and most misunderstood activity in the church. When the disciples asked Jesus to teach them to pray, I believe it was because they saw how prayer was to Jesus both a lifeline of relationship and a hotline of communication with the Father. Sadly, for many of us, prayer is only a helpline for solving problems.

Dr. Allan tries to correct or remedy this paradigm through a thoughtful and well-written book that aims to launch us not only into an accurate understanding of prayer but also ignite us with the spirit of prayer. If you do not wish to be ushered into a deeper realm of intimacy with God and effectiveness in prayer, read this book at your peril!

- Pastor C.N.S Prince
Snr Pastor, Revival Live Church. Dallas, TX

Get A Yes! comprises 40 percent personal examples, 30 percent of citations from his reading prowess of numerous erudite authors on Prayer, and the remaining 30 percent spiced with incisive apt Bible references. The depth of experiential knowledge in Get A Yes! makes the book very realistic and relatable and adds great value to the reader on this very important life activity of our walk with God.

It is said that information is power. Dr. Allan Olorunsola, in this well-articulated and deeply researched book, gives the reader very useful information needed to Get A Yes! in their daily spiritual duty of praying. Wherever you may be as a person of faith, this book will give you fresh insight. It is not possible to read Get A Yes! and not become more empowered as a Believer and trust that God is still in the good business of answering prayers.

- Pastor Williams Ekanem
Journalist, Author

GET A YES!

The Fundamentals of Answered Prayer

DR. F. ALLAN OLORUNSOLA

Selah Skript Publishing
Silver Spring, MD

Selah Skript Publishing
A division of Whitewall Media Consult LLC
P. O. Box 2568. Silver Spring, MD 20915
www.selahskript.com

GET A YES! The fundamentals of answered prayer.
ISBN 9798-9872022-0-3 (print)
ISBN 979-8-9872022-1-0 (ebook)

Printed in the United States of America

Library of Congress Control Number: 2022919820
First Edition, *Praying for Answers* series.
Unless otherwise indicated, all scriptures quotations are taken from the *King James Version* (KJV)
of the Bible

Scripture quotations marked as the following are taken from:

(NASB®) Scripture is taken from the New American Standard Bible®, Copyright © 1960, 1971,
1977, 1995, 2020 by The Lockman Foundation, used by permission. All rights reserved.
www.lockman.org"

(AMP) Scripture is taken from the AMPLIFIED® BIBLE, Copyright © 2015 by the Lockman
Foundation Used by Permission. (www.Lockman.org)

(AMPC) Scripture is taken from the AMPLIFIED® BIBLE, Copyright © 1954, 1958, 1962, 1964,
1965, 1987 by the Lockman Foundation Used by Permission. (www.Lockman.org)

(NKJV) Scripture is taken from the NEW KING JAMES VERSION®. Copyright© 1982 by Thomas
Nelson, Inc. Used by permission. All rights reserved.

(NIV) Scripture is taken from The Holy Bible, NEW INTERNATIONAL VERSION ®. Copyright©
1973, 1978, 1984, 2011 by Biblica, Inc.™. Used by permission of Zondervan

(GNT) Scripture is taken from the GOOD NEWS TRANSLATION in Today's English Version-
Second Edition Copyright © 1992 by American Bible Society. Used by Permission.

(NLT) Scripture is taken from the Holy Bible, NEW LIVING TRANSLATION, Copyright© 1996,
2004, 2007 by Tyndale House Foundation. Used by permission of Tyndale House Publishers, Inc.,
Carol Stream, Illinois 60188. All rights reserved. Used by permission.

(CEV) Scripture is taken from the CONTEMPORARY ENGLISH VERSION copyright© 1991,
1992, 1995 by the American Bible Society. Used by permission.

(ESV) Scriptures is taken from THE HOLY BIBLE, ENGLISH STANDARD VERSION ®
Copyright© 2001 by Crossway, a publishing ministry of Good News Publishers. Used by permission

(MSG) Scripture is taken from THE MESSAGE, copyright © 1993, 2002, 2018 by Eugene H.
Peterson. Used by permission of NavPress. All rights reserved. Represented by Tyndale House
Publishers, Inc.

DEDICATION

I would like to dedicate this book to the one and only "ABBA," the source and sustainer of all things. To the Jehovah El-Shaddai, who provides ready answers to all who call upon him. Thank you for filling our lives with testimonies of your goodness and your faithfulness. To the incomparable, immortal, invisible, the only wise God who daily loads us with his beautiful blessing, I say be magnified.

ACKNOWLEDGEMENT

I want to acknowledge the many people who allowed me to learn about the importance of prayer in the life of a Christian. Indeed, I would like to thank all the intercessors, prayer ministers, and the numerous Pastors, General Overseers, Bishops, and heads of fellowship for teaching me the art of prayer. I want to thank the members of Rhema Chapel Maryland-USA for all their love, patience, and support in completing this book. I also like to recognize the impact of my friends and colleagues in the ministry and the essential work of Prof. Patricia Agupusi, who did the major review of this piece on prayers. Equally, I appreciate the editorial prowess and dedication of Pastor Williams Ekanem, who did the book's final draft.

FOREWORD

Prayer, for the believer, is not only commanded; it remains an opportunity to connect with, walk with, and fellowship with God the Father, Jesus the Son, and the Holy Spirit. Thankfully, believers have the assurance of their prayers being heard and answered by a loving God who neither sleeps nor slumber.

Psalms 50:15 "Call upon me in the day of trouble: I will deliver thee, and thou shalt glorify me." God is a covenant prayer-hearing and prayer-answering God. He is committed to prayers as they are as incense in his nostrils. Therefore, if there is a man to pray, there is a God who hears and even does exceedingly abundantly above our anticipation, expectations and imaginations according to the power that worketh in us. Eph 3:20.

Despite the guarantee that we have of our prayers been heard and answered, praying just for its sake will not automatically produce the answer we desire and expect. This circumstance could be intriguing or surprising for many believers, some of whom have become frustrated and reduced or quit praying altogether. However, the scriptures cannot be broken; God hears prayer, however, prayer is an art, the fundamentals of which must be learned and practiced to get the right results. That God answers prayers doesn't mean He will do so as we expect all the time. God answers all prayers but isn't bound to always answer with a yes though that is what we expect all the time. That He chooses to respond in other ways apart from yes all the time doesn't mean He hasn't answered us, though. In respect of this, we find a scriptural foundation for Him answering a times with a No answer or with a yes but not now or with a different answer depending on what He believes is the best for us in our different situations. However, to get an answer to prayer, it must be approached in the right and proper, orderly manner as already given by scriptures. The throne of God isn't a place to come to in a disorderly fashion and expect an answer, though.

These many and other truth about getting answers to prayer is what Dr. Allan Olorunsola has x-rayed in this book "Get A Yes" Fundamentals of answered prayer. He has also emphasized the need to have an appetite for reading, meditating, memorizing, speaking and listening to the scriptures because one way to get answers to prayer is to pray in line with the word of God and this comes only when believers become word practitioner (having a working knowledge of the truths in the Holy Bible and doing them).

In this practical and practice-oriented book, the reader would certainly learn the purpose of prayer, their responsibilities in the place of prayer, as well as the steps they need to take in receiving the right answers to their desires from God. The readability and connection with the content is enhanced by Dr. Allan's strategic choice of words and usage of relevant illustrative real-life examples and stories to buttress the subject of discourse.

A journey through the seven chapters in the book will expose you to the simplest way possible to the Connotation of Prayer; Centrality of Prayer – The Holy Spirit; Concerning the Will of God; Connectivity in Prayer; Conditions of Prayer; Covenants of Prayer; and Confidence in Prayer.

I believe sincerely that a proper reading and study of this book would change a reader's understanding of prayer; therefore, this book comes highly recommended.

- **Rev. George Adegboye**
UK 2021

CONTENTS

INTRODUCTION

Right from many eons past, the human experience has been satisfied with the unique ability to call on the divine Supreme God in times of difficulties, challenges, and conflicts. While some people have had dramatic answers to their prayer requests, others, much to their chagrin, have been disappointed with the emptiness of not receiving a timely divine intervention or positive response whatsoever. In our modern-day living, the scenario of mounting challenges, difficulties, and conflicts has not changed. Now and then, we are challenged by situations that require the intervention of supernatural forces for victory or success to be assured.

The Holy Bible is complete with a plethora of man's encounters with the Divine God, who answers prayers. It is interesting to observe the process, criteria, and methodology with which this Supreme God answers prayers. This knowledge could help us navigate the uncertainties we might encounter when we find ourselves in a jam and when we need to reach out to the God of the Holy Bible in our moments of adversity, pain, and discomfort.

Prayer or the act of Prayer should not be conceived as an awful chore; rather, it should be as natural as breathing oxygen. The principles highlighted in this book are not supposed to represent a Prayer checklist but rather a practical guide. This prayer guide is purposed to be daily living experiences with the help of the Holy Spirit.

I believe it is God's paramount desire to answer every Prayer, we offer him according to his declaration in Jer 33:3: **"Call to Me and I will answer you, and I will tell you great and mighty things,**

which you do not know." (NASB). We see God intends to answer our prayers, but like everyone, there are times when we don't just get why our prayers are not answered.

This book is borne out of that concern. It is also a quest to understand why many prayers seem not answered and to highlight some of the missing spiritual landmarks. This writing, as well as its sequel in this *Praying for Answers* series, is a complementary book to the outstanding work of men and women of God who have given us incredible insight and understanding of the inherent power in prayers. As such, I will not be dwelling much on the different types of Prayer. I believe there are outstanding resources out there that deal with those topics. All the same, some of the issues will be mentioned just to give a contextual model and then move on to the missing elements.

On a broad spectrum, we have to realize that praying just for its sake will not result in getting an answer. Many observe that the act of receiving a positive response to Prayer could be somewhat mysterious. We can see two people pray the same seemingly prayers, and each gets a different experience out of that encounter. Why? You may ask, is God partial? I believe that God is not a partial being (Acts 10:34, Rom 2:11); however, the answers to our Prayer in many ways depend on the individual rather than God. This assertion about Prayer is what got me fascinated with this book. I could finally realize the between-the-lines nuggets essential to the business of answered Prayer, which is the goal of any Prayer petition or request.

We enjoy Prayer when we are continually praying with God's help. It is a daily experience, and I welcome you to enjoy the ride on this journey of discovery.

- **Dr. F. Allan Olorunsola**

CHAPTER 1

CONNOTATIONS OF PRAYER

Sandy, a registered nurse from Worster, Ohio, was diagnosed with a brain tumor. She was in a challenging situation at work and on the family front. She was trying to cope financially and emotionally with the demands of being a single parent. At the same time, her workplace didn't offer paid sick leave, so it was a double-hard period for her that was very difficult to bear. Her family took it upon themselves to organize prayer rallies across various denominations. She would later go for the surgery that lasted over 14 hours, and there were indications that Sandy might not make it. The prognosis was a disturbing development coupled with the scary fact that no one assisted the operating theater's neurosurgeon.

The precarious situation notwithstanding, her friend and family still gathered at the hospital to pray to the Almighty God, who answered prayers, and they got a yes! The surgery was successful, and she later left the hospital within eleven days. Sandy resumed her job three months after the surgery, and the finances worked out miraculously.

Just like Sandy, we all need to pray whenever situations or circumstances become dire or infinitely unpredictable. So, we pray when outcomes are uncertain, and the prognosis becomes bleak, but we still desire a positive response. To the military mother or wife, prayer is offered in the hope of a safe return of their loved ones from the war front. To the family facing dwindling financial capability, prayer is offered to bring about opportunities to earn more so that family can pay their bills. To the employee on the same wage for years, prayers are a platform to desire a significant increase in salaries and possible promotion.

To the single professional lady in her late twenties with many achievements yet no man in her life, prayer is expressed so that she can meet Mr. Right. This is also the experience of the high-achievement man expecting to meet the right woman. To the unemployed, prayer is sought so that there can be gainful employment. To the scientist working on a breakthrough vaccine for the Covid19 virus, prayer is concerted for a positive, actionable result.

To the married, still expecting to have their kids, prayer is offered for fertility and fruitfulness. To the medical student intern preparing for the medical board exams, prayer is considered to help to hope for the best. To the soccer players in the FIFA World Cup competition, prayer is offered for a successful winning outcome. To the graduating high school student, a high GPA, extra curriculum activities, internship, volunteering, sports, ACT or SAT scores; prayers are to get into the best colleges.

No matter who we are, what we are, or where we are, we all have weaved the wand of prayer more than we can remember. We have welded the rod of prayer in many diverse situations and circumstances. It is, therefore, authentic, in the words of Rev. George Adegboye, that *"The story of every great Christian achievement is the history of answered prayer."*

WHAT IS PRAYER?

The word prayer or, by extension, praying always conjures up various shades of meaning to people based on their understanding, knowledge, or experiences with the subject matter. No matter the white, black, or grey arrears of prayer, there are universal fundamental reasons why we all pray or should pray (for those not feeling this praying thing!).

First, let's just do an overview of what prayer means. I understand that in these days of modern Christianity, we might tend to view praying as that loud shouting in an attempt to get the supreme being's attention.

Yes, I know there are times when our voice gets louder, especially if you are dealing with some demonic issues and exerting spiritual authority. I understand that, but mere praying to God for basic stuff and shouting! Something is not all right. Apostle Leroy Thompson once said that "Real prayer is not a duty but an opportunity"

Let us look at what Webster's dictionary defines as a prayer so we can have a contextual frame of reference.

Prayer

- The act of offering reverent petitions to a deity; Any earnest request; A religious service made up mainly of Prayer; Something prayed for; A form of words appropriate to prayer.

The word Pray also means:

[2] Pray

- To address prayers to a deity; To make a request; To ask (someone) earnestly; entreat; To ask for by prayers or petition, and to affect by prayer

In context, the word prayer could mean so many things to so many people. However, culturally, it carries the same meaning in terms of the expected results. Archbishop Nicholas Duncan-Williams once emphasized in his book: *Forces Behind the Scene* that "Prayer is talking to God, and God talking back to you."

A couple of years back, my brother and his wife were selected for the Diversity Visa (DV) Lottery program. They were scheduled for the visa interview in Lagos, Nigeria. I spoke with him the day before the interview to confirm that they have everything in place. On the interview day, I got a call that the process was going differently than expected as there was some demand for clarifications and verifications.

These are some of the things that lead to visa denials on Passports. Uncertainty, fear, and doubt started settling in their minds. I felt uncomfortable and a little burdened by the information I was receiving. Since I was thousands of miles away on another continent, the only thing I could do was pray.

When I got their call, I was at work, so I had to take an early lunch break, and I went into my car to pray. I started petitioning heaven on their behalf for the process to be smooth and that everything would work out right. While praying, the Holy Spirit said," It is Done," and I felt a relief and a note of victory.

The next day, my brother called me to tell me of the good news that their visa had been approved and they were indeed on their way to relocate to the U.S. This testimony describes what Charles Spurgeon said, *"Prayer is able to prevail with heaven and bend omnipotence to its desire"* Praise God for answered prayers!

FUNDAMENTALS OF PRAYER

I sincerely believe that the best approach to any subject matter in Christendom is to view it from the perspective of Jesus Christ in the Bible. We must remember that all the religious acts and sacraments believers do today are not new. The Jews also had practiced all this even before Jesus showed up by the Jordan river. There's been much scriptural reading, praying, fasting, keeping the feasts, healing, miracles, deliverance, signs, and wonders.

Jesus didn't just come to continue these traditions but brought out the reality of all these practices. It's similar to getting used to the voice of a friend in another city we've not met in person. But when they show up in person, that is a different experience because we can understand their body language at a deeper relational level rather than the superficial voice recognition we are used to.

That is the same experience as what was going on before Jesus showed up on the religious scene. It was similar to the difference between a black and white TV set of the 1960s and the 8k UHD QLED colored TV of 2022! The olden days' black and white TVs are composed of cathode ray tubes (CRT), diodes, capacitors, and other parts to form a big TV box. Compare that to the 8k TVs nowadays in terms of electronics, colorimetry, and other physical attributes; it's like night and day. So, the Law and the religious traditions were going on before Jesus came preaching about the kingdom of Grace and Truth (John 1:18).

JESUS'S CONCEPT OF PRAYER (WHAT?)

Jesus made us aware of some hidden gems when He taught on Prayer in Matt 6:5-15. There are fundamental things Jesus revealed to us in all these passages – the Principles (What), the Purpose

(Why), and the Pattern of Prayer (How). Let's examined these basic principles now, and then we will consider more.

Principle #1 – The God-Given Right to Pray

Prayer is not a popularity contest of who can pray the best (Mat 6:5). Ephemeral standards should not weigh the efficacy of prayer. God will answer prayer not just because an anointed individual (Pastor, Pope, Bishop, Prophet, Evangelist, Elder, Deacon, Apostle) prays but simply because he is a prayer-answering God. Ps 65:2 says, "**O You who hear prayer; To You, all flesh will come (NKJV)**'. God is the God of all flesh, and by creative rights, He is compelled to hear every man, woman, boy, or girl. To Dana Williams in Benton, Maryland, a stay-at-home mum at the time with their year and half old daughter, prayer indeed connote surprise.

She and her husband lived in a house with a small yard and wanted a sandbox for their baby girl, but their budget could not accommodate it. This mother and her little daughter prayed, asking Jesus to send them a sandbox. Three days later, the husband came home from work surprisingly with a sandbox in the trunk of his car. His boss decided to give him a sandbox from the extra their family had.

Principle #2 – Prayer is a Personal Dialogue

Prayer is not about how we are perceived in the public eye (family, church, neighbors, Pastor) as praying men or women. It is a personal dialogue between an individual and God (Mat 6:6). Considering this, it is irrelevant to letting people know how many hours we pray or how many days we fast. The main essence is to connect with God and let him hear you and answer you.

During this writing, I decided to go on a three-day fast, but God provided answers to all my requests by the second day. I fasted from 6 am to 6 pm. Even then, my wife didn't know. I just got myself in the study, and my family thought, oh! He's studying, don't disturb him. I do not need to announce to everybody, oh, I'm going on a three-day fast, Blah! Blah! Blah! That's just taking the spiritual shine out of the whole experience. The Lord Jesus cautioned us not to let the public know that we are fasting by our demeanor (Mat 6:16-18).

There was a story of a barren woman in the bible who suffered much ridicule from her rival. The woman, Hannah, was provoked to her breaking point limit that she simply refused to eat. Yes, there are times when vexation and dissatisfaction could make us lose our appetite. At the yearly Shiloh festival, she unloads her heart's burden before the Lord (I Samuel 1:10 – 18).

Hannah asked God to give her a son and promised to give the Son back to the service of God. While she was praying, only her lips moved, but there was no sound coming out of those lips. All her requests were formed in her heart, yet God heard and gave her a son. The central point is that loud voice or not, shouting or not, God will always answer prayers!

Principle #3 – Prayer is Not Repetition

The next principle is that Praying is not about the number of words we speak or how often we repeat them to God that determines the outcome (Mat 6:7). A father who asks his son what he wants for Christmas does not need to hear the request repeatedly. Well, sometimes, kids try to be complicated by their dramatic reminders. We must accept that our heavenly Father knows the things we need before we even ask. Isa 64:24 says:

"And it shall come to pass, that before they call, I will answer; while they are yet speaking, I will hear (KJV)"

This third principle of Prayer Jesus talked about suggests that God knows everything we need or will become. By implication, there is no need to get on continually asking God for things the ordinary person wants. I don't want us to take this principle out of context by suggesting that there is no need for prayers since God knows what we need. It's like singing along with Doris Day in his song: "Que Será, Será" (whatever will be, will be). We can also apply basic human reasoning to this and say if God already knows what I need, why do I still ask? Why can't He just go ahead and give it to me?

In his Book: *Men of Like Passions*, Rev. George Adegboye said, "Prayer opens the limitless storehouse of God and introduces those who practice it to the world of unlimited privileges. It brings the strength and wealth of heaven to the aid of ordinary men." Yes, prayer is not a repetition, but we need to ask still.

THE PURPOSE OF PRAYER -WHY PRAY?

Everyone on earth has a different desire at one particular time or the other. When it comes to God answering our prayers, we must wrap them with an essential ingredient – being specific. This definiteness will bring us to the fourth principle Jesus taught about Prayer in Mark 11:24 **"Therefore I say to you, whatever things you ask when you pray, believe that you receive them, and you will have them."(NKJV)**

Principle #4 – Desire

Every time we pray before God, there must be a burning desire in our hearts. This desire translates into a focused request that helps us to be consistent with what we want. We see Jesus demonstrate this principle often when people come to Him for healing or a miracle. He is always fond of asking them, "What do you want me to do for you?" I know that to some, that statement might come like a shocker. Imagine the blind Bartimaeus, who had to go through many obstacles to get the attention of Jesus. He finally got his chance when Jesus asked him to come (Mark 10:46-52).

I believe Jesus is not oblivious to Bartimaeus's blindness, but He wasn't sure of "What" he wanted. He could have come to ask for alms. Bartimaeus could have happened to discuss a religious issue he had been talking about with his fellow beggars. He could have come to talk about how his Father's family has neglected him and not taken care of him and probably would like Jesus to be the judge. There is a plethora of reasons why Bartimaeus wished to see Jesus. In the same terrain as believers today, it is important to articulate our heart's desire before we even get to church or the place of prayer. It is not just a wish list but a burning passion. Anyway, Bartimaeus finally got to Jesus, and he was asked that destiny-changing and straightforward question, **"What do you want Me to do for you" (Mark 10:51) (NKJV).** Bartimaeus could only say, "I want to see."

After I succeeded in passing my University (College) entrance exams and was offered Engineering, it was time for the verification exercise at the admission office. The lady checked my results then credentials and decided that the school wouldn't grant me college admission because I had one of my names missing on one of the documents. I explained that I had an affidavit by my father to attest to the change of names. She flatly refused. There was a lot of back and forth, and time was running out with classes commencing and exams scheduled. I finally lost that admission.

However, through prayers and the Holy Spirit's comfort towards my desire to study Engineering, I had to reapply the following year. I found myself going through the same verification process. The same lady who had refused to sign off on my admission documents gladly and willingly completed the admission process, and I could enroll in my desired Engineering program. Whatever the situation or circumstances, the Lord wants us to have pinpointed desires when we pray. We need to show Him where we want him to rain his answers.

Dr. David Yonggi Cho, who co-founded the world's largest Pentecostal Christian Church in South Korea, shared this prayer experience in his book: *The Fourth Dimension*. At the start of his ministry, he asked God for three things: a table, a chair, and a bicycle. When Dr. Cho observed that there seemed to be no answers to prayer, he began asking God why? The Lord made him understand that he wasn't specific enough. The table and chair would need to be identified based on the type of wood material. Also, God wanted to know the kind of bicycle he desired – American-made or locally made. Once Dr. Cho could identify the type of table, space, and bike he wanted, he got a speedy answer to his petition.

We must understand that before we approach God, we must know that He does not operate based on assumptions. We must tell Him exactly what we want. The Gospel singer Kirk Franklin once said that "God can only heal what we reveal." Equally, God is not moved by our feelings but rather by our faith, belief, and trust in His ability. It makes so much sense that Heb 11:6 would command that: **But without faith, *it is* impossible to please *Him*, for he who comes to God must believe that He is and *that* He is a rewarder of those who diligently seek Him (NKJV).**

While Jesus emphasizes that sometimes we need specificity and definiteness for our prayers to be answered, He also mentioned forgiveness as another valuable nugget in that same **Mark 11:25-26. "Whenever you stand praying, if you have anything against anyone, forgive him [drop the issue, let it go], so that your Father who is in heaven will also forgive you your transgressions and wrongdoings [against Him and others]." (AMP).** This divine requirement brings us to the fifth principle of prayer.

Principle #5 – Forgiveness

One of the reasons we need to pray is that it provides us the platform to forgive others. There's a saying by Alexander Pope, "To err is human; To forgive is divine." Forgiveness is not one of the human character strengths because it will require us to let go of the blame, accusation, pain, shame, atrocity, anger, resentment, and in many instances, animosity. From the natural human point of view, this is a hard thing to do. We can consider a traumatic situation such as when a young child witnessed his parents murdered or abused. Or you find unscrupulous people lying and sabotaging your interest in a business deal. We could also find ourselves at the whims of people who persecute, backbite, use, defame, and disrespect us. Other human situational predicaments tend to bring people to their low points. We see people's feelings all torn apart and in emotional turmoil because they can't phantom the depth of the pain and shattered dream.

As a young boy of eleven, I desired a bicycle because most of my mates in our neighborhood had one. I learned the price to get a fairly used one and started saving towards my bike. I had saved the money needed to purchase one, so I told my uncle about my plan to get the bicycle, and he obliged by saying he'll help me buy it. I gave him the money, but he never purchased the bike nor discussed what he did with my money. I became sad, dejected, and hopelessly inconsolable at the gravity of such misfortune. He thought it was just a childhood fantasy.

Still, back then, it was a shattered dream, disappointment, and quenching the satisfaction of being able to ride with my friends. It was a painful experience that made me harbor hatred and unforgiveness toward my uncle. Later in my teenage life, I realized through God's grace that I needed to release such people from my heart and forgive past hurts, pain, shattered dreams, and broken hearts. I had to forgive my uncle for the huge disappointment he had caused me.

I have come to recognize the art of forgiveness when it takes place. Usually, this togged in my heart when I thought about someone who had hurt or caused me pain, embarrassment, or disrespect. As humans, this sense of loss is the legitimate strand for payback, revenge, resentment, and ultimately avenging the harm or injustice done to us. Even though this legal right to avenge wrong is real, there is another thing in the play – the presence of the Holy Spirit.

As new believers, we are encouraged to walk in the Holy Spirit's fullness that dwells within us. So, when I switch to my heart's frequency, I can sense God saying you must forgive and release the person from your heart. Then I ask God to forgive me for holding the person in a grudge, and then I say something like", Lord, I forgive so and so, and I release him from my heart." Each time I go through this process, I perceive how God sees the offending person.

In prayer, we can release the pain, guilt, shame, anger, resentment, and hatred towards any person who has caused such emotional unrest. Frank Damazio succinctly stated it in his book: *The Power of Spiritual Alignment* that "Forgiveness is what we do to clean our hearts so that Jesus Christ can occupy His rightful place there. Forgiveness can restore the present, heal the future and release the past." This attitude is where God can do a transfer between His Spirit and our emotions. This state is where we can truly be free from those emotional pains and receive a fresh supply of hope, joy, gratitude, trust, belief, and a merry heart. Ps 50:10 -12 say:

> *Create in me a clean heart, O God, And renew a steadfast spirit within me. Do not cast me away from Your presence, And do not take Your Holy Spirit from me. Restore to me the Joy of Your salvation, And uphold me by Your generous Spirit (NKJV)*

King David in the Bible is someone who, in many ways, symbolized the worst thing that could happen to a person in terms of pain, persecution, hurt, rejection, disappointment, fear, shame, betrayal, and hatred. He would later write a lot of Psalms about these trying times. His escape from king Saul, the betrayal of his Son, Absalom, and the people were planning to kill him. Yet in all these, David still found a way to let it all go so he could fulfill all God had in store for him. He had a perfect understanding that it is what we receive from God that we can give to others.

I understand the scar will still be there because of what they did, but the attitude will be to do them good rather than evil. One sure way to ascertain if we've genuinely forgiven someone is to go to them when we have an explicit opportunity to harm, disappoint, or hurt them. We become clothed with the Spirit of forgiveness. I think forgiveness is the ability that God grants us to live above the pain, the hurt, the disappointments, the failure, and the resentments.

The act of forgiveness is like breathing, where we can breathe in the love of God and breathe out the Spirit of forgiveness. The atmosphere of prayer is the perfect environment for forgiveness to take place. It's no surprise Jesus tucked forgiveness within the boundaries of prayer. Until God gives us Joy, there is no way we can provide it to others.

David said in Ps 16:11: **You will show me the path of Life; In Your presence is fullness of joy; At Your right hand are pleasures forevermore (NKJV).** Joyce Meyer is an anointed teacher of God's word who tells us the untold pain, hurt, and disappointment she experienced after being sexually abused by her father for many years. But God later healed her through this ordeal, and she forgave her dad for all he did. It was a challenging, unpleasant mission to accomplish, but with God's help, she could forgive her dad.

During Prayer, God can overwhelm our hearts with His everlasting love, and that flow is what supernaturally enables us to release people who have wronged or hurt us. In this milieu of divine Joy, we can find it in our hearts to finally forgive others without any regret or remorse. Wow! I'm feeling the love of God right now. Let's just go ahead and ask Him to fill our hearts with His fullness of Joy.

Let us then release and forgive anyone who might have hurt, despised, persecuted, or caused us untold harm, shame, hardship, or other wrongdoing. This seeming cooperation with God is needed to express and experience forgiveness, and there wouldn't be any blockage of answers. There is also another area in that God requires our cooperation, and this leads us to the Sixth basic principle of prayers:

Principle #6 – The Jurisdiction of Prayer

The more we think about the concept of prayer, the more we realize the many somewhat legal elements involved. Jesus admonished us in Luke 18:1 about the Prayer Continuum when he said: **Then He spoke a parable to them, that men always ought to pray and not lose heart (NKJV).** The Apostle Paul also echoed this principle in 1 Tim 2:8: **I desire, therefore, that the men pray everywhere, lifting up holy hands, without wrath and doubting (NKJV).**

Many ministers in the Word of Faith movement always refer to the statement made by John Wesley, founder of the Methodist Church, that "the Almighty God can't do anything on earth unless someone, somewhere, asks Him." In Ps 115:16, the Bible shows that: **The heaven, even the heavens, are the Lord's; But the earth He has given to the children of men (NKJV).**

When God made Adam, He gave him the planet earth's lease as the resident custodian or manager (Gen 1:26-28; 2:5-8). But sadly, Adam sold out that lease to the Devil when he disobeyed God, and then everything went south for the human race.

So, it takes a man or woman, for that matter, to send a request that will permit and authorize God to move on planet earth. Even when God had promised the coming of the Holy Spirit in Joel 2:28-32, Jesus still had to pray to the Father for the release of the Holy

Spirit in John 14:16: **And I will pray the Father, and He will give you another Helper, that He may abide with you forever (NKJV).**

Yes, God is omnipresent and omnipotent, but He can't violate the laws of the earth. He needs the cooperation of man for any spiritual progress on earth. We can observe that prayer is as old as the first generation of settlers on Earth. It shouldn't surprise us that Gen 4:26 will say that: **At that [same] time men began to call on the name of the Lord [in worship through prayer, praise, and thanksgiving] (AMP).** So, they knew the importance of prayer, which is the ability to activate and release the ability of God's power. All these bring us to the concept of jurisdiction, and we will discuss this further in Chapter 7.

In the book of Acts, chapters 1 and 2, we see an exciting development. Jesus was letting the disciples know that there was a God-given promise of the Holy Spirit that empowered them to be effective witnesses. However, we also see the disciples gathering in the upper room to pray for this promise to be fulfilled. They didn't feel it would automatically come to pass without engaging the prayer instrument. The disciples continued in prayer until the day of Pentecost was fulfilled, and they were all baptized in the Holy Ghost and began speaking in tongues.

We need to know exactly what the approximate 120 people were praying for. Some Christians believe we need to tarry and seek the Holy Spirit's baptism, just as the disciples did at the beginning of the book of acts. I just want to make one thing clear from the scriptures. The disciples were not praying just to speak in tongues; they were praying for the Holy Ghost season (era). Let's put all these scriptures in proper perspective.

1. **And I will pray the Father, and He shall give you another comforter... John 14:26 (KJV)**

2. How God anointed Jesus of Nazareth with the Holy Ghost and with Power...Acts 10:38 (KJV)
3. But you will receive Power when the Holy Spirit comes on you... Acts 1:8 (NIV)
4. I will pour out of my Spirit on all people... Joel 2:28 (NIV)
5. When the day of Pentecost came, they were all together in one place. Suddenly a sound like the blowing of a violent wind came from heaven ....Acts 2:1-2 (NIV)

Summarily, we noticed a person of the Holy Spirit and a power dimension of the Holy Spirit. Also, the personality dimension comes before the evidence of power manifestations. We must take cognizance of the fact that there is just one day of Pentecost in Acts Chapter 2, but there are many instances of believers being filled with the Holy Spirit with the evidence of speaking in tongues without the so-called waiting period (Acts 8:15-18; 9:17-18; 10:44-46; Acts 19:3-7).

The day of Pentecost means the era or the period of the Holy Spirit. We are in that era; it has happened. Therefore, we don't necessarily need to tarry for days to replay the day of Pentecost; neither do we need to wait to be baptized with the evidence of speaking in tongues. We can just simply ask God in faith, and He will fill us with the Holy Spirit.

All these crucial aspects of the Holy Spirit's empowerment happened because people prayed, and God responded. The scriptures teach us in James 5:16; **The heartfelt and persistent Prayer of a righteous man (believer) is able to accomplish much [when put into action and made effective by God – it is dynamic and can have tremendous power] (AMP).**

Let us examine the events when the early Christians suffered persecution for believing in Jesus Christ. King Herod imprisoned Apostle Peter after killing James. Acts 12:5 says: **So Peter was kept**

in prison, but fervent and persistent prayer for him was being made to God by the church. (AMP). As a result, an angel appeared suddenly in that prison and brought out Peter. What a mighty deliverance! No matter what the enemy meant for evil, it can and will be averted through heartfelt, continuous prayers. Archbishop Nicholas Duncan-Williams summed it up perfectly "prayer assassinates the enemy's plan and turns everything in your favor."

I remembered one of my sisters in the Lord when God revealed that the Devil planned to kill her before her 50th birthday. So, I stood in the gap to pray and intercede on her behalf, proving her case before the Lord that the scriptures say she would live to see her children's children (Ps 128:6). Secondly, He promised to satisfy her with long Life (Ps 91:16) and that she would live and not be supposed to die at the young age of 50 (Ps 118:17). After Praying for some time, I got a note of victory and heard the Lord say to me," She Shall live" She is still alive today and living well because someone prayed. Yes, we pray to enforce the rulership, dominion, and fulfillment of God's will on earth. Praise the Lord!

Principle #7 – Fullness of Joy

There are no parents out there that do not want to give the best things to their children. Parents want their kids to be joyful and happy. It is also an inherent nature of God to make our joy to be full by simply answering our prayers when (a) they are filled with a desire, (b) flows in forgiveness, and (c) makes His power available. Jesus said in John 16:23-24:

> *And in that day you will ask Me nothing. Most assuredly, I say to you, whatever you ask the Father in My name. He will give you. Until now, you have asked nothing in My name. Ask, and you will receive that your joy may be full. (NKJV).*

From these seven principles, we have discovered the different shades of meaning of prayer and prayer's essential purposes. When we grasp the "what" and the "why" of prayer, we can easily translate that knowledge into practical know-how. We are now moving into the practical aspect of prayer. Jesus showed us the many "How" of Prayer in His teaching about prayer. We look at the very first significant pillar of how to pray.

Principle #8 – The Name of Jesus.

An individual's name is the most significant representation of who they are and the kind of respect or power they command. Our names are unique and represent our power, authority, aspirations, attributes, characters, and potential. All authority in the universe is invested in the name of Jesus Christ (Phil 2:9-10). The name of Jesus has power and authority in three realms of existence – Heaven, Earth, and under the earth (Mat 28:18). This inherent power in Jesus's name made him declare in John 14:13-14: **And whatever you ask in My name, that I will do, that the Father may be glorified in the Son. If you ask anything in My name, I will do it (NKJV).**

Some time ago, while making a company trip to one of our client's locations in Silver Spring, Maryland, I had a severe stomach cramp. I was about to get out of the car when it started, and I was about fifteen minutes to my appointment. The sensation I was having was like having food poisoning, where body coordination is difficult to maintain because you are too concerned about clutching your stomach. I started playing with the possible scenarios. I could call 911, cancel the appointment, and arrange for someone to pick up my car.

Alternatively, I could put what I know about prayer into practice. Well, I decided to go with the latter option, so while still grabbing my abdomen, I started declaring, "in the name of Jesus Christ of

Nazareth, I command everything that is not okay with my stomach to become normal. I take authority in the name of Jesus and speak to my stomach to function in the right way it was created to operate." After some 5 minutes of standing in my declaration's faith, I started getting relieved from the stomach cramps, and I could complete meeting the business client.

The name of Jesus Christ is readily available to every child of God. E.W Kenyon states that "the right to use His Name is a conferred blessing to the Church – it is a right that belongs to every child of God" Jesus assured us all in John 16:23: **And in that day you will ask Me nothing. Most assuredly, I say to you, whatever you ask the Father in My name. He will give you" (NKJV).** The name of Jesus is what grants us the authorization for answered prayers. We see the Apostles in Acts 3:6-8, depending on the validity of Jesus's name:

> *"Then Peter said, "Silver and gold I do not have, but what I do have I give you: In the name of Jesus Christ of Nazareth, rise up and walk." And he took him by the right hand and lifted him up, and immediately his feet and ankle bones received strength. So he, leaping up, stood and walked and entered the temple with them—walking, leaping, and praising God." (NKJV).*

With Jesus's name, we can perform signs and wonders (Mk16:17-18). Evangelist Reinhard Bonnke said, "Prayer in Jesus's name is always to make the will of God possible."

Jesus showed us the many "How" of Prayer in his teaching about prayer. Let us look at other principles as highlighted in Math 6:9-15; let us understand how the principles can be employed in our everyday living experiences.

Principle #9 – Approach the throne with gratitude (vs. 9).

We are encouraged to come into God's presence with gratitude in our heart. The scripture says in Ps 100:4, **we should enter his gates with praise and into his courts with thanksgiving.** The element of praise creates an atmosphere of joyfulness, and it allows our hearts to be engulfed with God's possibilities. In this state, our problems and difficulty seem to lose their grip on us. Praises make us acknowledge the supreme authority of God (Ps 103:19).

Principle #10 – Desire first, the fulfillment of God's will and intentions (vs. 10).

One key element in effective communication is having other people's interests at heart. I believe Jesus also imbibed these expectations about putting the interests of God first. He emphasized this as a very strategic key to getting prayer results. He said in Matthew 6:33, **"But seek first the kingdom of God and His righteousness, and all these things shall be added to you." (NKJV).** The kingdom of God entails His approved right way of doing things. We must learn how to act right towards our neighbors, people, and those above us in authority or ranking.

Principle #11 – Make a demand for divine provision and supply (vs11)

God, the Father, indeed knows everything we need, but He still wants us to ask Him for the specific things we need. I believe God wants all His children to be happy, and one way to achieve that is to give us exactly what we want when we want it. As parents, we always have a pretty idea of what our kids want. But then we rely on their judgment to make an informed choice of something they want. This peak of the pack selection will give them their greatest joy. God is relating to us in the same way and wants us to choose the top priority things we want. He has assured us in John

16:24: **"Ask, and you will receive, that your joy may be full."** (NKJV)

Principle #12 – Flow in forgiveness (vs12)

Sometimes we get offended by family members, co-workers, friends, or people. This little confrontation could escalate into a shouting match that often leads to anger, resentment, and frustration. Later during the day, we would want to pray, but we discovered we couldn't do it. Why? We feel the emotional disconnect, which lets us know that prayer is not only a magic wand that we can weave over things or situations, shouting "Abracadabra." It is such a moment of human vulnerability that the comforter, the Holy Spirit, would remind us of the need to let forgiveness flow before even asking anything. It is the divinity of God in man that makes us instruments of His goodness.

Principle #13 – Recognize God is the only supreme power (vs. 14)

This last principle pivots on the idea of a singular focus. What we set our eyes on determines what flows towards us. It is either our focus on God or someone or something else. This dependency on God allows us to eliminate any alternatives that could make us entertain doubt. James 1: 6-8 says,

> *But let him ask in faith, with no doubting, for he who doubts is like a wave of the sea driven and tossed by the wind. Let not that man suppose that he will receive anything from the Lord; he is a double-minded man who is unstable in all his ways. (NKJV).*

TYPES OF PRAYERS

While we've been able to see Jesus teaching us about the fundamental pillars of prayer, in terms of the "What," "Why," and the "How" of prayers, it will also be utterly essential to acknowledge the different kinds of prayers, prayer is like sports, where there are different kinds with unique sets of rules. The rule of Soccer does not apply to the game of Basketball or Tennis. In the same way, this differentiation also applies to various types of prayers. Let's see some of the salient characteristics of these diverse kinds of prayers.

1. Prayer of Praise and Worship – This type of prayer is offered more in Psalms' book. The main objective is to focus attention on what God has done and who He is.
2. The Prayer of Faith is to change situations or circumstances. The authority of the believer activates it. James 5:16
3. The Prayer of Consecration – the prayer of total commitment to God's divine plan and purpose.
4. The Prayer of Binding and Loosing – exercising spiritual authority over the enemy of God's people.
5. Prayer of Casting Cares – A deliberate decision to allow God to help us through mounting pressures.
6. Prayer of Supplication – Petitioning God to meet our needs.
7. Prayer of Agreement – The coming together of two or more people to agree on a prayer plan.
8. Corporate Prayers – A place where a group of people gathers to pray about issues that concern everybody jointly.

Everyone will agree, to some extent, that prayer is a means of getting the desired outcome, irrespective of the premise or assumptions we may have about the perceived results. This dialogic participation between God and individuals makes prayer a real supernatural force. Apostle Leroy Thompson once commented that "if you spend time in prayer, God will do something supernatural for you" In the book of 2 Kings 5:10-14, we see Naaman, a Syrian Captain having leprosy and in dire need of God's divine intervention to get rid of it:

> *And Elisha sent a messenger to him, saying, "Go and wash in the Jordan seven times, and your flesh shall be restored to you, and you shall be clean." But Naaman became furious, and went away and said, "Indeed, I said to myself, 'He will surely come out to me, and stand and call on the name of the Lord his God, and wave his hand over the place, and heal the leprosy.' Are not the Abanah and the Pharpar, the rivers of Damascus, better than all the waters of Israel? Could I not wash in them and be clean?" So he turned and went away in a rage. And his servants came near and spoke to him and said, "My Father, if the Prophet had told you to do something great, would you not have done it? How much more then, when he says to you, 'Wash and be clean'?"*
>
> *So, he went down and dipped seven times in the Jordan, according to the saying of the man of God; and God restored his flesh like the flesh of a little child, and he was clean (NKJV).*

Naaman's concept of calling upon God for healing was based on expecting some theatrics from the Prophet Elisha. He assumed that with just some abracadabra gibberish, God would just heal him. How wrong were those suggestions or perceptions? We often think prayer is just saying anything in prayer and expecting God's obligation to answer, even if it violates some of His characteristics. To some people, as long as they get the answer, that is all that matters. We need to understand some divine ground rules to answer prayer.

THE GROUND RULE FOR PRAYER

We must understand that prayer's main essence is to reach out to divinity so that there can be a significant change in our natural circumstances or situation. It is to bring to bear the supernatural power of God to bail us out. In her book: *Beyond The Veil,* Dr. Alice Smith said concerning prayer, "The child of God will touch the heart of God, bask in His loving words of affirmation, tremble at His unlimited power and authority, and come away forever changed." We should also know that God reserves the right to who has access to the use of His supernatural resources.

We must realize that there is a divine WILL concerning the things of God. Yes, God is so particular about His will that the bible emphasizes in Ephesians 1:11:

In whom also we have obtained an inheritance, being predestinated according to the purpose of Him who works all things after the counsel of His will: (NKJV)

All things are done according to God's plan and decision (GNT)

The Bible explains that God will not even move or do anything without the explicit consent of His own will! That is an earnest assertion we must also grasp with all seriousness to see our prayers answered. The Rev. Kenneth Hagin says prayers cannot be effective until God's will be clearly understood.

Without knowing God's will in the particular subject area, it would become a trial-and-error basis or merely a rolling-the-dice process. In the book: *Prayer-The Neglected Ministry of Jesus,* Pastor Sola Fabunmi commented that "if you do not actively seek God's will, you will never experience total satisfaction."

THE FATHER'S WILL

One of the important subjects of interest to Jesus Christ is fulfilling His Father's will. Some might say, what has the Father's will got to do with anything? I just want to pray and get the results I want. We need to realize that the whole world is ensconced in God's will in terms of the spiritual, physical, and cosmic realms. So, we must take a cue from Jesus and grasp the importance of knowing God's will in any situation.

After settling in the U.S. for over a year, my wife and I decided to purchase our first home – a two-bedroom Condo apartment. For a couple new in the country, that could be a challenge, mainly if you apply for a mortgage. You must have a good income and a good credit rating. Well, I had a good job, but we had not built up enough credit, but we applied anyway. The lenders were asking for so much documentation and coupled with the fact that there were other bidders for the property with more established credit, the situation was uncertain.

Finally, the bank approved our mortgage application, but we were second on the list because the seller decided to go with another buyer. We were looking forward to moving to that particular area in Maryland. It would have been perfect accommodation, and the mortgage amount was almost equivalent to renting an apartment. As God would have it, the loan officer called me and told me that the first bidder couldn't close the deal for some reason or another and that I should push in my bid.

Even though there was the issue of insufficient credit, we still went ahead to put in the bid for the condo and forgot about it. Afterward, as I was praying about the whole accommodation thing, the Rhema word of the Lord came, quoting Isa 34:17b "They shall possess it forever; From generation to generation, they shall dwell in it." Wow! I felt on top of the world, and I just began blessing the faithfulness of God. I felt the burden lifted and had a tingling upbeat note of victory in my heart. I was happy because I sensed God was working something out. The answer to prayer manifested in the next couple of days as the loan officer called me to come to pick up the key and then complete the closing documentation process. Hallelujah!

I believe God desires His children to live fulfilled, satisfying lives. The will of God is what I summed as: **The Original Intention of God.** God never created anything just to have fun only. He never made anything without a purpose or a function. Everything in life occupies a place for a divine assignment. We all have a specific divine purpose of accomplishing a destiny on Earth. We see God's clarion intention in Genesis 1:26-28

> *Then God said, "Let Us make man in Our image, according to Our likeness; let them have dominion over the fish of the sea, over the birds of the air, and over the cattle, over all the earth and over every creeping thing that creeps on the earth." So God created man in His own image; in the image of God He created him; male and female He created them. Then God blessed them, and God said to them, "Be fruitful and multiply; fill the earth and subdue it; have dominion over the fish of the sea, over the birds of the air, and over every living thing that moves on the earth. (KJV)*

From the above text, we know that there are just four primary intentions for every man or woman on earth. These are God's original intentions.

- **Fruitfulness** – Productivity, Creativity, Success,
- **Multiplication** – Increase, Prosperity, Abundance
- **Subdue the Earth** – Inventions, Solutions, Innovation

- **Dominion** – Earth's Manager and Controller.

The Bible is also replete with the original intention of God concerning every daily issue of life, ranging from marriage, work, relationship, salvation, friendship, success, family, leaders, children, parents, money, giving, widows, righteousness, justice, judgment, sin, and so many more.

God's original intention is often made known by the specific words He says or gives through His servants. God's original intention also deals with the purpose or, in a contemporary language – His Push Button. Tellingly, God's Will is His original intention, words, purpose, and Push Button. So, putting this in a pseudo framework, we see that:

God's Will = His Intention = His Words =
His Purpose = His Push Button

THE FATHER'S WILL AND JESUS

We see this recurring theme about the Will of God throughout the Life of Jesus Christ. We need to know that Jesus was the quintessence of answered prayer. Everything He prayed for; He got an answer! We can see several differences if we compare how Jesus prayed and how believers are praying these days. While these differences might not be in the approach or the language, there are notable differences in the outcome.

There are some things Jesus knew instinctively, and He was in the habit of putting these things into daily practice. If we can only grasp some of these things, I'm confident we would have outstanding results, just like Jesus. Considering the simple definition of God's will, let's look at the effect this has on the life and ministry of Jesus, our pattern.

Jesus's Birth

Some hundreds of years before the birth of Jesus, many Old Testament Prophets foretell about His coming. These Men of God were all stating the original intention of God. In Isaiah 7:14, the scripture says: **Therefore, the Lord Himself will give you a sign: Behold, the virgin shall conceive and bear a Son, and shall call His name Immanuel. – Isaiah 7:14 (NKJV).**

Also, in Isaiah 9:6, the word of God shows us that:

> *For unto us a Child is born, Unto us a Son is given; And the government will be upon His shoulder. And His name will be called Wonderful, Counselor, Mighty God, Everlasting Father, Prince of Peace.*

> *Of the increase of His government and peace There will be no end, Upon the throne of David and over His kingdom, To order it and establish it with judgment and justice From that time forward, even forever. The zeal of the Lord of hosts will perform this. (NKJV)*

We see the fulfillment of these prophecies when the Angel of the Lord appeared to the parents of Jesus, Joseph (Matthew 1:21), and Mary (Luke 1:26-38). Jesus was born to fulfill a God-given mandate to save the whole human race from eternal judgment and destruction. Even when there were threats to His physical Life, God made a way to see that no harm came to His only begotten Son.

Jesus's Ministry

Jesus started His ministry by acknowledging that the presence of the Father is with Him. He demonstrated this right from His baptism in the River Jordan, where He asked John the Baptist to baptize Him, and when He went about healing many (Mat 9:35). Jesus was always concerned about fulfilling His Father's will. In the classical rendition of the Lord's Prayer in Matthew 6:9-15, Jesus requested that God's will be done on earth as it is in heaven (Mat 6:10 NKJV).

We can recall from these scriptural backgrounds that Jesus was doing all that was purposed for Him to accomplish by healing, delivering, and saving people (Matthew 4:23; Act 10:38; Galatians 1:4; I John 3:8). In His earthly ministry, Jesus was so engrossed about God's will that He said that anyone that would just do it would be considered a bother, a sister, and a mother! (Mark 3:35)

Jesus Death

The crucifixion of Jesus was something that the Lord had planned and conceived before the world began (Revelation 13:8). He pursued the will of God irrespective of what was coming against Him (Psalms 40:8, Hebrews 10:7). When the hour for His demise came, Jesus was so burdened about the next phase of His purpose, so He went to a place called Gethsemane to intercede for His soul prayerfully. (Mark 14:32-42). He took a prayer point to God that we see in Mark 14:36 - **Abba, Father," he cried out, "everything is possible for you. Please take this cup of suffering away from me. Yet I want your will to be done, not mine." (New Living Translation NLT).** We see a very troubling encounter here as Jesus began to experience the full realization of the weaknesses of the human nature he bore.

He had performed miracles, healed the sick, and raised the dead. Jesus, the anointed messiah, had preached to the masses and worked wonders among His people. He had commanded the wind to stop and walked upon the waters. He had prayed for Lazarus, and God heard that prayer as He had always provided answers in the past (John 11:41-43).

Jesus had demonstrated absolute faith in God and expected all believers to have the same God-kind of Faith (Mark 11:22-24), assuring us that once we believe, all things would be possible for us (Mark 9:23).

But at this stage in Jesus's Ministry, a pre-planned event needs accomplishing – He must die.

Jesus found Himself with two mutually exclusive options. On the one hand, He could harness God's unlimited power through the instrument of prayer to turn the grave situation around. On the other hand, He could simply submit to accomplishing God's will. Jesus started with the prayer of faith and reminded God that all things are possible with Him. But at the end of that rather very intense prayer session, Jesus showed us that the answer to prayer lies in fulfilling the Father's will. It will always supersede any Prayer possibilities. God will always side in with His will, not necessarily His rules and principles, which are derivatives of His original intention. God's purpose is to express what He says and declares, and they are not subject to change (Numbers 23:19, Psalms 89:34, Isaiah 55:11). The foremost thing in the heart of Jesus was to please the Father by doing His will.

PAUL'S PRAYERS

We see this pattern of unflinching conformance to God's will and purpose in the life and steadfastness of Apostle Paul, who wrote approximately two-thirds of the New Testament by God's grace. He is a unique individual who vested his heart's desire in understanding and fulfilling God's will. Apostle Paul was so engrossed in it to the extent that when faced with persecution, he confidently said in Acts 20:24:

> *But none of these things move me; nor do I count*
> *my life dear to myself, so that I may finish my race*
> *with Joy and the ministry which I received from the*

> *Lord Jesus, to testify to the gospel of the grace of God. (NKJV).*

This sold-out attitude burdened Apostle Paul, who desired that believers know and understand God's will in every situation.

> *For this reason we also, since the day we heard it, do not cease to pray for you, and to ask that you may be filled with the knowledge of His will in all wisdom and spiritual understanding (Colossians 1:9, NKJV);*

Again, we see the Apostle Paul admonishing the believers at Colosse:

> *Epaphras, who is one of you, a bondservant of Christ, greets you, always laboring fervently for you in prayers, that you may stand perfect and complete in all the will of God (Colossians 4:12, NKJV);*

Also,

> *I have not stopped giving thanks to God for you. I remember you in my prayers and ask the God of our Lord Jesus Christ, the glorious Father, to give you the Spirit, who will make you wise and reveal God to you, so that you will know him. I ask that your minds may be opened to see his light so that you will know what the hope to which he has called you is, how rich are the wonderful blessings he promises his people, and how very great is his power at work in us who believe. (Ephesians 1:16-19, GNT)*

While thinking and wondering about this "Will of God" business, we need to read the Bible and be aware of some facts or what they call "Caveat Emptor" in legal terms. Yes, it is highly essential to read and study the scriptures and apply them correctly (2 Timothy 3:15).

Dr. Fred K.C. Price once said that "everything in the bible is truly stated but that not everything is a statement of truth" We read in the bible stories, opinions, encounters, and experiences of people in their dealings with God. Are these personal meetings somewhat applicable to our lives today simply because they are written in the Bible? How do we differentiate the real truth from just the opinions of men? To spot the difference between the truly stated and statement of truth dilemma, I always like to bring up a well-known scripture in Job 1:21.

And he said: Naked I came from my mother's womb, And naked shall I return there. The Lord gave, and the Lord has taken away; Blessed be the name of the Lord. (NKJV).

I know we've all heard the famous quote from the Bible during the burial of a loved one or when circumstances become unfavorable. Then we see people pulling out this scripture as if it's a soothing balm and portends that whatever the dire situation, it's God's perfect will, so we need not worry. Notwithstanding, it does not matter how long we've heard or believed those words from the lips of Job; it is not in line with God's original intention. Let's look at it in the light of telling the statement of truth from an opinion that is truly stated.

STATEMENT OF TRUTH

A Statement of Truth

- is always consistent with God's nature and character (good, righteous, just, love)
- it is backed by God's Power (2 Pet 1:3-4, Heb 1:3, John 6:63);
- it is eternal (Isa 55:9-10, Ps 119:89, John 1:1-4, I Pet 1:23);
- it will always produce faith (Rom 10:17)
- it saves, heals, and delivers (Ps 107:20, Rom 1:16)

A Truly-Stated idea or Opinion

- It is not consistent with God's nature or character.
- It is always based on environmental factors and hence subject to change.
- It is forever embedded in connotations and ambiguities.
- It is borne out of uncertainty and does not produce faith.

It is for our benefit to differentiate the difference between the opinions and statements of men in the Bible from the expressed will of God. This ability could sometimes mean the thin line between life and death when we are in a situation; we are not sure it indicates God's will.

We must remember something about God's will: it does not change. God's will for man is in all goodness, righteousness, and mercy. He is always and will forever be known as Jehovah the Good (Jer 29:11). The will of God still flourishes in an environment that does not change. It is an environment that is governed by the laws of the Spirit (Rom 8:2)

CHAPTER 2

CENTRALITY OF PRAYER: THE HOLY SPIRIT

If there is one thing we can pinpoint as the main central thing about getting answers to prayers, it is the Holy Spirit's influence. Prayer will be like playing the lottery without him; it will just become another game of chance. People will waste precious hours and days thinking they are praying but not knowing they are praying amiss. In the book: *You Can Hear the Voice of God*, Steve Sampson said, "Prayer is not cerebral; it is birthed. Real Prayer is not repetition; it is following the Holy Spirit."

We should not see the Holy Spirit as a tool or equipment in our prayer arsenal. Rather, we should see Him as He is: the third person in the Holy Trinity of God the Father, Son, and the Holy Spirit." The Holy Spirit is the one thing I'm sure of in this book, and He is authentic.

My first encounter with the Holy Spirit was over three decades ago as a teenager finishing high school. At that time, I had gained the freedom to begin to decide how I wanted my life to become. I had become fascinated with the artistic prowess of Michael Jackson, and I was trying to model my persona on him. I started buying his music and some famous pop singers of that era. Back then, my sister used to share the gospel with me, and once in a while, I'd come to

Christian gatherings where they would preach and make the invitation to be saved. I usually decline such invitations with the excuse that I am not ready. This stance of mine used to frustrate my elder sister, and I seemed more deeply involved with my friends, who were not making any positive progress in life. But the truth was that the whole gospel was not practical to me. It seems like an abstraction from the planet Mars.

GET BORN AGAIN

Then came the Holy Spirit on that faithful night as He suddenly awoke me. I heard Him as if He was speaking behind me and said, "Why don't you get born again?" At that question, I started ranting about the whole salvation thing being a religious farce. I believed in the things I could touch, see, observe, and analyze back then. I explained that I didn't see any real power in this so-called idea called the gospel. Then I heard the Holy Spirit say, "Get born again, and I will show you the power behind the gospel." The thought of that statement warmed my heart and made me accept as I went on my knees, asking God to forgive me and accepting Jesus as my Lord and savior.

The minute I prayed that prayer of salvation, I felt relief; it took a burden off my shoulders. I felt an overwhelming emotion of love (Romans 5:5), and all I could sense was a feeling of being righteous and good. This sensation of goodness instantly replaced all my ill feelings and evil thoughts toward people. I didn't have any urge to lie or behave as in my past persona. I felt precisely what 2 Cor 5:17 declares: **Therefore, if anyone is in Christ, he is a new creation; old things have passed away; behold, all things have become new (NKJV).** My change was so drastic that my sister and my parents immediately noticed something had happened to me.

The Holy Spirit started unveiling things to me from the scriptures. I began to get revelations and visions about God's purpose and plan. I was growing in the sincere milk of the word of God and my relationship with the Holy Spirit. I discovered that I knew things supernaturally without people telling, preaching, or trying to convince me of anything. But an incident happened that will somehow change my understanding of spiritual things.

On the 8th of March 1986, I lost my mum in a car accident. She had gone to see her dad, my granddad, concerning the arrangement for his ordination as a Bishop. On the way back, her taxi had a head-on collision with another vehicle. The passerby's rushed her to the general hospital with a head injury. I'm overwhelmed by the nostalgic feeling of my loving mum, and I miss that woman! What a loss I had experienced at that young age.

Here is what I want to extract from that painful event. Throughout that day, I had a witness or an urge that something was wrong. I couldn't put my finger on it. I don't know what it was, but I believe the Holy Spirit was trying to let me know what would happen. I wasn't knowledgeable about praying, interceding, exercising authority, etc. All I had was just a witness that something was amiss. While the whole family was in high spirits that my mum would arrive that day, it was apparent we were all missing her. I was not in high Spirits because something terrible was bothering me.

Yes, when we become believers, we are born of God's Spirit, allowing us to know things supernaturally. Anyway, I kept pacing the house until I heard the phone ring. It was as if a fire hose had gone off within me the minute that happened. It was as if I should just go ahead and tell my dad what the call was. There was a knowing that something terrible had happened to my mum.

My dad dropped the phone and became silent. He called my uncles and other family members to get to the hospital. They started making the necessary arrangements and kept the kids in the dark, but I knew something bad had happened to my mum. If I had the essential knowledge about praying and interceding, I could have stood in the gap and prayed her through. There were so many questions about why this. Why that? How did it happen? I knew this was not God's perfect will for us. The enemy might set his attacks, but we must take authority over this in Prayer with the Holy Spirit's help. Not long after this experience, I enrolled in what might be considered a school of the Spirit. God started teaching me about His leading and the responsibility that goes along with that leading. He taught me about the efficacy of a Rhema word versus the written word (Logos).

The first Christian book I was opportune to read as a believer was Rev. Kenneth E. Hagin's book, titled: *How To Be Led By The Spirit Of God*. The book gave me a framework for what the Holy Spirit was doing in my life. I had the same revelations, encounters, and experiences described in that book. It was quite a delight to read it because it seemed like I was writing my biography. After all, it is the same Holy Spirit (2 Cor 4:13). That is why I stress this Holy Spirit aspect in our Christian experience because it could sometimes determine the outcome of a life-death situation.

Jesus made us realize that the Holy Spirit is the most outstanding personality in our lives, and we would be delving into a bit of His person, purpose, ministry, leading, and guidance.

THE PERSON OF THE HOLY SPIRIT

The Holy Spirit is the third person of the Holy Trinity's Godhead and has the same attributes as God the Father and God the Son (Acts 5:3-4, 1 Cor 12:4-6, 1 Pet 1:2). He is omnipresent (present everywhere), omnipotent (all-powerful), and omniscience (all-knowing-John14:26). He is also eternal (Heb 9:14) and sovereign (Zech 12:10).

Dr. Lester Sumrall said, "if God's Holy Spirit is to function fully in our lives, we must have an open heart and a consuming desire to know all we can learn about the nature and role of the Holy Spirit" The Holy Spirit has been in operation on earth ever since its inception in the Gen 1:2. The earth was without form and void, and darkness was on the face of the deep. And the Spirit of God was hovering over the face of the waters. He has been operating more in a higher dimension since Jesus's resurrection. The Holy Spirit is not a wind, dove, force, fire, water, or anointing oil; He is a Person!

The Holy Spirit has similar characteristics nature of a person (John 6:63). Let us look at the character traits of the Holy Spirit. He has a mind (Rom 8:27); He witnesses (Rom 816, John 15:26); He Speaks (John 16:13, Acts 1:16, 8:29, 10:19, Heb 3:7-8, 1 Tim 4:1, Rev 2: 7, 11, 17, 29); He searches all things (1 Cor 2:10); He can be grieved (Eph 4:30); He has a will (1 Cor 12:7-11); He can be resisted (Acts 7:5); He loves (Rom 15:30); He teaches (Luke 12:12, John 14:26, 1 Cor 2:13); He is a counselor (John 14:26). There is a creative power dimension of the Holy Spirit, but that is not my focus for now, but we want to look at its primary purpose in the believer's life.

THE MINISTRY OF THE HOLY SPIRIT

Jesus specializes in one thing: He will always give us the foundational truth (John 8:32). No wonder Apostle Paul concluded in 1 Cor 3:11 that: **For no other foundation can anyone lay than that which is laid, which is Jesus Christ (NKJV).** For this purpose, Jesus taught us through three chapters (John 14 – 16) about the ministry of the Holy Spirit as it relates to His mission and function.

The Holy Spirit is called the comforter according to **John 14:16: And I will ask the Father, and He will give you another**

Comforter (Counselor, Helper, Intercessor, Advocate, Strengthener, and Standby), that He may remain with you forever (AMPC) I just want to reiterate some of the things I shared in the first chapter. The Holy Spirit didn't just come of His own accord; Jesus had to pray to the Father to send Him. I wish to stress the importance of asking and receiving prayer dynamics. Nothing about God is a game of chance.

In the Greek language, comforter means Parakletos. There are seven expressions of that word, which is what we can expect from fellowshipping with the Holy Spirit. So, we can receive Counseling, Help, Intercessions, Advocate (pleading on our behalf), Strength, and Standby (residual power) from the Holy Spirit.

I went shopping one day for some slip-on shoes, and while I was looking at the displayed items, I heard the Holy Spirit say, "Why don't you buy one for so and so (he mentioned the name of the brother)" So I said OKAY, and I bought the extra pair of shoes. When I got home and gave the shoe to my brother, he was surprised and asked how I knew he needed that shoe. He said he was thinking about getting one of those shoes for himself, and I had bought it for him. His answer came because I'd obeyed the prompting of the Holy Spirit.

We must note that when the Holy Spirit asks us to do something, we should respect and value His opinion even when it does not make logical sense. We need to acknowledge that He knows everything and can see much further into our future than we can remember our past. This attitude will keep us grounded and humble to accept His leading gladly.

THE FUNCTIONS OF THE HOLY SPIRIT

Jesus talked about the Holy Spirit's eight functions in John 14:16-17; John 14:26; John 15:26; and John 16:7-14. These are (1) Abide with us, (2) Teach us all things, (3) Bring things to our remembrance, (4) Testify of Jesus, (5) Convict the world of sin, righteousness, and judgment, (6) Guide us into all truth, (7) Show us things to come, and (8) Glorify Jesus. Every day we wake up, the Holy Spirit wants to perform these functions. Along with these functionalities are the kind of nature or influence He has over the believer. We see the importance of the Holy Spirit as it relates to:

- Power (Act 10:38, Act 1:8, Micah 3:8)
- Salvation (John 3:5-6)
- Fruitfulness (Isa 32:15)
- Love (Rom 5:5)
- Knowledge, wisdom, and understanding (Isa 11: 2, Job 32:8, Ps 51:6)
- Liberty and deliverance (2 Cor 3:17, Isa 61:1, Isa 10:27)
- Transformation (2 Cor 3:18)
- Excellence (Dan 6:3)
- Sanctification (1 Cor 6:11, Heb 9:4)
- Ministry Gifts (1 Cor 12:7-11)
- Prosperity (Deut 8:18)
- Supply (Phil 1:19)
- Glory (I Pet 4:14)
- Grace (Heb 10:29, Zech 12:10,

THE LEADING OF THE HOLY SPIRIT

I have mentioned many instances where I said the Holy Spirit said this or told me that. I want to talk about how He leads and guides us. I have equally discussed the scriptural foundation of the personality, ministry, nature, and the Holy Spirit's function. The discussion is meant to imbue our faith and trust in God's word about the Holy Spirit. It is a yardstick to measure our expectations and subsequent experiences with the Holy Spirit.

In his classic book: *You Can Hear the Voice of God*, Steve Sampson observed, "True spiritual growth doesn't transpire until the believer begins to hear from God." In essence, the more we can hear from God via the Holy Spirit, the more we grow spiritually. Hearing from God must not be construed to mean hearing strange voices but rather identifying and discerning his promptings (Rev 2:17).

There are many ways the Holy Spirit can give us spiritual guidance. While some are the primary way, others are sometimes one-offs. Two foundational scriptures point to this aspect of the Holy Spirit. Prov 20:27 says, **"The spirit of a man is the lamp of the Lord, Searching all the inner depths of his heart" (NKJV).** Romans 8:14 says, **"For as many as are led by the Spirit of God, these are sons of God" (NKJV)**. These two scriptures tell us that every child of God should expect to be led through their spirit man.

God is primarily interested in relating with us through our spirit man, not our head, emotions, and feelings. The spirit man is that new nature we have when we got saved (2 Cor 5:17). That is the person that got born of the water and the Spirit (John 3:5-6, I Pet 1:23), and that is the being that gets baptized in the Holy Spirit (Act 1:8, I John 4:4). So here are some of the ways the Holy Spirit leads or speaks to you.

INWARD WITNESS –URGE, CHECK, HUNCH

One fundamental way God said He would guide us is through the inner witness, hunches, urges, or conscience. Rom 8:16 says, **"The Spirit Himself bears witness with our spirit that we are children of God" (NKJV).** How do we know that we are saved, born-again children of God? There is an inward sense of assurance or conscience. We don't know how to explain it entirely, but we just know beyond any doubt that we are saved. Even if someone might start arguing this fact with us, we might not be able to convince them logically, but there is just that deep-seated knowing. It is similar to our conviction about the names we bear. No one can convince us that we are not the names we bear. The more we consider that inner persuasion, the stronger it becomes. Sometimes, it could seem like a hunch or gut feeling, but it will always be in line with the Holy Spirit's peculiar nature. I shared the witness I had about my mum's accident even though I was in a different environment.

I usually attended a youth prayer meeting during my earlier years of learning to follow the Holy Spirit's leading. After the prayers, we would all form a circle by joining hands, and the leader will ask someone to do the closing prayer. All the while, we have our eyes closed. I observed that whenever I'm supposed to round up the prayers, I usually feel excitement inside (I later understood this as the Holy Spirit's unction or enabling). While the last prayer point is coming to a close, I would get a tap on my shoulder to round up the group's Prayer. I just have that hunch, gut feeling, and knowing I would be doing it.

The more I began to depend on that inward witness, the stronger and better it became. But the Holy Spirit will always start with the little things to train our spirit man before graduating us to the other more significant issues in our lives, such as whom should I marry?

What career should I pursue? What ministry should I join? What is God's calling upon my life?

There are signs to look out for when being led by the inward witness. Sometimes, it will seem like you are getting information from two sources: one comes from your inner man and the other from your intelligent mind. You must realize that your inner man or spirit man is the real you, and it is the creature that houses the Holy Spirit.

The inner man knows many things that our head or intelligence can't understand because it continually communicates with the Holy Spirit. Here we are spirit beings because we are made in God's image and likeness, and God is a spirit (John 4:24). Secondly, our spirit man will always bear witness to the truth because of the influence of the Spirit of truth. The truth deals with the reality of God's word in the light of the situation, thereby making us side with what is right. What this means is that we need to feed (train) the new man with the sincere milk of the word of God (1 Pet 2:2) through reading, meditating, and listening (Rom 10:17).

One benefit of being led through the inward witness is absolute clarity about what to do next. Luke 4:1 says, **"Then Jesus, being filled with the Holy Spirit, returned from the Jordan and was led by the Spirit into the wilderness" (NKJV).** About two years ago, I was in the kitchen trying to get some food from the refrigerator into the microwave. At that instant, I just had a witness to go on a two-day fast. It is only the usual 6 am-6 pm fasting, and I don't know what the Lord wants to do. So, I packed the food back into the refrigerator and went about my business.

The purpose of fasting, to me, is to be able to concentrate more on some things. Back in college, I used to do what I call fast and read, especially during semester exams. I will forgo eating and delve into reading, and I noticed my concentration and assimilation rate increase tremendously. I still practice this tradition today. When I'm engaged in cerebral activities, I find eating difficult until I have completed the task. Fasting also sharpens our spiritual sensitivity to quickly grasp what God might tell us.

Anyway, I was fasting for the first day, and as I was getting ready to close from work, I got a call that one of the Hotels my company supported was experiencing a system downtime. A system outage completely shut down their Wi-fi network. I was on the call that week, so I had to check it out. I drove some forty minutes or so, and as I got to the outskirt of that city, I sensed that God was giving us another property in that area of Maryland. I got to the hotel, still trying to wrap my head around what the Lord had just witnessed in my heart.

While waiting for the systems to come up, I checked my emails and got a house notification in that area that met my ideal dream house. Later that day, the Lord started sharing with me the revelations He gives believers. He said there are always two screens of sight that we can look at concerning anything. God said there is a natural (physical) sight and a supernatural (invisible) sight. That is another discussion for another book, but I got a divine direction for the particular city we will be moving to. God is always interested in guiding us in every detail of our lives. Ps 37:23 says: **"The steps of a good man are ordered by the Lord, And He delights in his way" (NKJV).** The Holy Spirit gives us an added advantage to differentiate what is real from what is a sham. He helps us know what will work for us or not.

THE INWARD VOICE OF THE NEW MAN

The real, new spirit man on the inside is the real person. The person we see in the mirror is just a replica of that real man on the inside. The inner man has a voice and speaks or repeats what he picks up from the indwelling Holy Spirit. Let's understand this process. Jesus said the Holy Spirit would not speak of Himself, but He would receive from Jesus and then speaks what He receives (John 16;13). The Holy Spirit will receive the word of God. Any leading from Him will always be in line with the scriptures.

I want to also talk about the principle of equivalence here. This principle is that the quantity of God's word in our spirit man will determine the amount of what the Holy Spirit can show, teach, or guide. It is the truth we know that we can work in (John 8:32). The Holy Spirit is somewhat limited without the word of God. God's word is His truth (John 17:17), and the Holy Spirit will guide you based on the truth (word).

You must have an appetite for the scriptures – reading, meditating, memorizing, and listening to them. We become word practitioners by having a working knowledge of the truths in the Holy Bible. For the first three years after I was born again, I had the luxury of reading the Bible in so many ways (topical, chapters, books, memorizing, sermonizing, etc.). I was also listening to teaching ministers. After getting the word into our hearts, we need to cultivate it by acting on the word we know.

This process is like exercising our spiritual muscles. It might be awkward at first. For instance, you heard the bad news, and the natural thing that comes to mind is organizing a pity party and getting all the "I'm Sorry" gifts. However, the Holy Spirit might remind you of specific scriptures contrary to your circumstances. Some verses like, **In everything give thanks for this is the will of God in Christ Jesus for you (I Thess 5:18, NKJV); Rejoice in the Lord always, again I say rejoice (Phil 4:4, NKJV); My brethren, count it all joy when you fall into various trials (James 1:2, NKJV).**

Our mind might want to prevail and make us act according to our situation, but if we just decide to act according to the Rhema, we will become spiritually strong. I John 1:7 says, **"If we walk in** the light as He is in the light, we have fellowship with one another, and the blood of Jesus Christ His Son cleanses us from all sin" (NKJV).

All this is necessary because it is from the Logos that the Holy Spirit will bring out a Rhema or spoken word that will bring solutions to the particular issue we might be facing. Jesus said he would bring to our remembrance the word.

The voice of the Spirit is as if someone is speaking behind you, but it is coming from your spirit, man, and we hear it with our inner ear. I will share more about this in subsequent chapters, but the scenario is either of two ways. We get a direct quote from the scripture that deals with our situation. We could also get a statement or an instruction on what to do, which will still be in line with the scriptures. When the word comes, it brings so much peace and assurance. Some years back in 2002, while preparing for my wedding ceremony, I met with my Pastor, who told me that the officiating minister might not come.

There was another wedding scheduled at the same time in the Headquarters church. As soon as my Pastor delivered the message about the conflicting schedule and the possible postponement of our time to the afternoon, the Holy Spirit said, "He shall not fail, neither be discouraged." That was a direct quote from Isa 42:4. So I just received the word of the Lord concerning the situation. Then, the other family suddenly canceled the so-called wedding at the headquarters church, and the Bishop was available to officiate at my wedding. We didn't change the schedule because God had already said the plan would not fail, and it didn't!

VOICE OF THE HOLY SPIRIT

The only difference between our inner man's voice and that of the Holy Spirit is that the latter is more authoritative. It is more audible

(Louder) than the previous methods; it is to get the full undivided attention and is more prevalent in the Old Testament. Even though they were not saved nor their spirit man reborn, God could still speak to them. You just instantly know. God does not need to live in people and things to talk to them. In so many ways, we see where the word of the Lord came to the patriarchs of old.

When the Holy Spirit speaks, it's more compelling, and there is no mistaking that God is the one speaking to you. You just instantly know. Ps 29:3-4 declares:

> *The voice of the Lord is over the waters; The God of glory thunders; The Lord is over many waters. The voice of the Lord is powerful; The voice of the Lord is full of majesty (NKJV).*

The audible voice of God varies in intensity, just as we can control the volume of a loudspeaker. So, God can speak in a whisper (1 Kings 19:12) or in normal talking range (Gen I2:1, I Sam 3:4-9, Acts 26:13-16), and he can also speak in a thunderous manner (Exo 19:18-19, Rev 1:10, Rev 14:2).

It was during my second year (Sophomore) in college. I was done for the day and just slept off, and then suddenly, I found myself in a life-like dream. In that dream, I found myself bound with chains with another man in a cage amid a witch's coven. I could see the bonfire in the center on the ground from the cage and the leader wearing a black hood. One of the people came to the holding enclosure, picked the other man, and took him to the leader.

This leader used him as a sacrifice, and all I heard later was his cry of anguish. I observed that I was out of my physical body, had all my senses intact, and knew it would be the end of me. I thought about people waking up the next day and realizing I couldn't wake up. They would have many hypotheses about people dying in their sleep. I played that scenario in my mind as I was held captive in that cage. I also noticed that I had become mute, and my mouth felt gagged even though I didn't see any tangible element tied across my mouth.

The rituals at the coven continued, and it was my time to be offered to the leader. One of the lieutenants came to pick me up from the cage, and then we walked toward the leader. I tried to fight my way, kick, shout, and do all I could, but it was futile. I was filled with sorrow, knowing that it would be the end of my existence. It would be saying goodbye to my family, friends, and loved ones who had put their hope in me. I felt hopelessly helpless, and at that moment, I succumbed to the dire situation's reality. We finally arrived some four feet from the leader. So, the leader turned, and as he stretched out his hand to grab me, I shouted and screamed JESUS! I caught a glimpse of what happened next; it was as if someone had dropped a bomb in that place.

I could get the sensation of massive destruction. While all this was happening, I observed that I was getting back into my body in my room at the student hostel. I opened my eyes, and the sweet Holy Spirit said, **"That which is born of the flesh is flesh; and that which is born of the Spirit is Spirit"(KJV).** Of course, that was a direct quote from John 3:6. The Holy Spirit started ministering to me that there is no witch, wizard, occult, or any power that can harm or do anything to me because I'm born of His Spirit. **I John 4:4 says, "greater is He that is in us than he that is in the world."** Rom 13:2 says**," there is no power but of God, and the powers that be they are all ordained of God,"** Ps 62:11 says that **"Power belongs to God."** I was also trying to remember what the Lord told me the day I was getting saved, that He would show me the power that accompanied the gospel. The gospel is the power of God unto salvation (Rom 1:16-17). Whenever I think about this incident, I'm always grateful to the Holy Spirit for His great deliverance from untimely death.

OTHER METHODS OF LEADING

Yes, the Holy Spirit will always lead, help, and guide us as much as He can. While those three methods we described above are the primary fundamental ways the Holy Spirit communicates with us, there are different ways. The first one is the written word (Logos). Sometimes you are reading the scriptures, and it seems like a particular bible verse is emphasized more than usual. The scripture appears somewhat alive, and you begin to get insight or revelation from that verse. This oomph seems to come over you as you just think about the scripture. That is God speaking to you.

God does speak to us also in dreams and visions. Joel 2:28 shows us that:

> *And it shall come to pass afterward That I will pour out My Spirit on all flesh; Your sons and your daughters shall prophesy, Your old men shall dream dreams, Your young men shall see visions. (NKJV).*

A year after getting married, we still believed God to have kids. We were unaware of any medical conditions that would deter those expectations, yet; there was nothing to show for it. I was not worried about this, believing it would happen at the appropriate time. On one faithful night, the Lord showed me a vision of our firstborn's birth certificate. The certificate had his full name (first and middle name).

Please understand that anything God shows, He can always bring to pass by Himself. I got up from bed and thanked God for His will to be fulfilled. That vision finally came to pass some four years later when my wife got pregnant. Then, my wife jokingly teased me, saying, "what if the first child was a girl." I told her that's not what God showed me.

God has been using dreams and visions to speak to people from the word go. Abraham (Gen 12:7), Jacob (Gen 46:2), Joseph (Gen 37:5), Daniel (Dan 2:19), Solomon (I king 3:5), Ananias (Acts 9:10), Peter (Acts 10:19), Paul (Acts 16:9-10, 18:9). There are other ways God also speaks to us, such as the gift of prophecy (I Cor 14:3-4), other gifts of the Holy Spirit (Word of knowledge, word of wisdom, tongues, and interpretation of tongues (1 Cor 7:4-11)), other ministry gifts in the body (Apostles, Prophets, Teachers, Pastors, and Evangelists – Eph 4:11-13)

DEVELOPING THE CAPACITY TO HEAR GOD

It is pertinent that believers continuously build their capacity to hear from God. Amid contrary evidence, emotional upheavals, and distractions, we must maintain the discipline to hear fresh from heaven. One of the very sure ways to develop the ability to listen to God is to pray in the Spirit (tongues). Apostle Paul said in **1 Cor 14: 2, 14,**

> *"For he who speaks in a tongue does not speak to men but to God, for no one understands him; however, in the Spirit, he speaks mysteries...For if I pray in a tongue, my spirit prays, but my understanding is unfruitful".(NKJV).*

The fastest way to build spiritual sensitivity is by praying in the Holy Spirit. **Jude 20 says But you, beloved, building yourselves up on your most holy faith, praying in the Holy Spirit (NKJV).** If you are not baptized in the Holy Spirit, I will advise you to do that ASAP. When we become filled with the Spirit, we have the full potential to be led by the Holy Spirit.

About the tail end of 2019, I started thinking about some of the church administrative tasks that need completion. We had registered the church as a North American non-profit organization, but we have a Maryland flagship operational base. I was not comfortable paying for another registration in Maryland. That will entail double payment and processing for everything we have now. So, after some praying time, I just heard the words "dba," which is a term used in business entity registration for "doing business as" I later went online to check it out. I sent the application to the secretary of state, and it all worked out. They would allow us to legally have the two entities operating with the same credentials. Praise the Lord!

God is always looking out for us. He is interested in everything that concerns us: physical, financial, mental, health, and marital. Whatever God shows or says to us, we have a responsibility to dare to believe to the extent that we take a corresponding action in line with it. Every dealing with God on every level still needs to meet that universal requirement of having faith in him (Heb 11:6). He wants to meet us on the prayer platform.

Our Intentions

Someone might be asking if it's true God would talk to me. The answer to that question is a big Yes. The Holy Spirit wants to speak to you daily because He is inside of you 24/7. He wants to answer every question we have in our hearts. When the Lord speaks, it does not follow our natural human mind's logical activity, which merely follows what it wants to communicate at that time.

I want to drop some final thoughts on all this: voice, vision, dream, and God's leading. First, we are not seeking that God should speak to us in a particular way or method. He knows how we are wired, and in His wisdom, He would decide the best way to communicate with us. The method does not matter; that does not make it supernatural or spiritual. As long as the Holy Spirit does it, it will be useful and impactful.

I always thought of what Kenneth Copeland would say about the leading of God. He always says that he has never heard God's audible voice, only the inward voice in his heart. That's how God decided to deal with him; he has impacted the world.

The second point I want to draw attention to is that no matter the Holy Spirit's leading, it will always align with the word of God (Truth). The leading will always align with God's will, which in every indication is the word of God. This precaution is necessary because other voices, visions, prophecies, and dreams are not from God.

This disclosure brings me to the third nugget. We can judge or discern whether a particular leading is from the Holy Spirit. Anything from God will first bear a witness with our Spirit; after that, it will produce joy; then there would be peace about it, and it might inspire us to take a step of faith. Above all, there will be that serenity of the outflowing love of God. However, if, on the other hand, there is fear, condemnation, uncertainties, and dampened troubled Spirit, we need to take heed and stay clear. We shouldn't be carried away with the spectacular but endure to remain sensitive to only the Holy Spirit, and we will always get a yes!

CHAPTER 3

CONCERNING THE WILL OF GOD

In the preceding two chapters, we've established a ground rule that must be observed for God to intervene in our petitions and the necessity of the ministry of the Holy Spirit. We pointed out that we need to differentiate the real truth from the opinions or good ideas of men and God's availability to lead us toward the right answers. There is no other more significant kingdom requirement than for believers to pray. Jesus expressed His intention for us to pray without ceasing (Luke 18:1). Apostle Paul also urged us to pray all the time with all manner or types of prayers. The common denominator in any kind of Prayer is the will of God. In light of this assertion, Apostle Paul admonished believers in Ephesians 5:17:

Therefore do not be unwise, but understand what the will of the Lord is (NKJV). The wisest man, King Solomon, revealed this expectation some thousands of years past in Proverbs 4:7: **Wisdom *is* the principal thing; *Therefore* get wisdom. And in all your getting, get understanding (NKJV).**

We are all concerned about getting a grasp of the will of GOD. Whether in life, marriage, family, ministry, career, business, or life. There is always that question of "is it God's will?" Sometimes, when I get involved in some projects and sense opposition or resistance, it is much easier just to throw in the towel and say, "maybe it's not God's will." The more I think deeply about what I'm doing in the light of what the Bible says in Ps 1:3c, **"And in whatever he does, he prospers."(NASB),** the better insight I gain to stick with the project. The level of difficulties does not determine the yardstick to measure if an idea or event is God's will. Jesus went through difficult times as a preacher that contradicted the religious traditions of his days. He also went to the cross, a suicide mission, yet it was all part of the will of God. We need to understand the will of God for our lives, family, community, and nation. That is when we would then be able to live according to a purpose.

I want to submit that God's will is His original intention, expressed word, purpose, thoughts, and push button. Furthermore, God's will is His delight, desire, plan, decision, pleasure, ideas, decree, and choice for an individual, family, group, community, or nation. Jeremiah 29:11 shows us that:

For I know the thoughts that I think toward you, says the Lord, thoughts of peace and not of evil, to give you a future and a hope (NKJV). God's will are His expressed thoughts and purpose in the holy scriptures.

ENFORCE GOD'S WILL

We must realize that understanding God's will in any situation is crucial to getting our prayers answered. Some months after moving into our new house, I felt this restlessness and was troubled in my spirit. It was as if some evil force was trying to influence some things in the environment. I was upset. After all, I needed to sleep and couldn't, which I found strange because I didn't have difficulty sleeping. I sat in bed, leaned forward, and started praying and taking authority over my house and the environment. I commanded any outside evil force to leave in Jesus's name and enforced every promise God made concerning me and my home. After doing this, I waited some sixty seconds to let all the prayers sink into my conscious and subconscious being and went back to sleep. I was confident that no evil force could go contrary to what I had declared because it was the expressed will of God.

I understood God has to ordain perfect peace for us (Isa 26:3,12, John 14:27, 2 Thess 3:16, Phil 4:6-7). He also declared that my habitation would be peaceful (Isa 32:18), and no evil will come near my dwelling (Ps 91:10). Archbishop Nicholas Duncan-Williams Once said that "said prayer brings out of eternity into time, the original intent of God"

So, I have a divine responsibility to enforce the will of God over my situation and environment. Jesus said in Mat 6:10: **Your kingdom come. You will be done on earth as it is in heaven (NKJV).** We are spiritual legislators that enforce that God's intention and purpose be accomplished in our lives, families, community, and nation. We must know and understand God's will in all areas of our lives.

Rev. Kenneth Hagin used to say that victory in Prayer is not guaranteed until God's will is known. We must realize that God is mostly about His purpose, and that is what will always stand the test of everything, including answers to prayers (Isa 14:24-26). The Apostle John made this fact of God siding in with His will more pronounced when He said in I John 5:14:

Now this is the confidence that we have in Him, that if we ask anything according to His will, He hears us (NKJV).

At this junction, I would like to mention two essential Nuggets about God's Will:

1. God's will is revealed through His expressed intentions in the Bible concerning issues such as:

- Salvation – John 3:16, I Tim 2:1-4

- Healing – Math 8:17, I Pet 2:24, Ps 107:20.
- Forgiveness – Eph 1:7, Col 1:14, I John 1:9
- Blessing – Eph 1:3, Gal 3:14
- Long Life – Ps 91:16,
- Deliverance – Col 1:13
- Prosperity/Success – Joshua 1:8, Job 36:11, Ps 35:27, 3 John 2
- Fruitfulness – Gen 1:26-28, Ps 1:3, Deut 28:11, Ps 92:14
- Increase – Ps 71:21, Ps 85:12, Ps 105:24, Ps 115:14, Eze 36:12
- New Birth/Creature – 2 Cor 5:17, John 3:5-6

2. God's will is only predicated on His truth, and it protects us from lies of the Devil (Ps 91:4). Earlier, we highlighted the difference between a statement of truth and an opinion that was truly stated. No matter the number of people saying or making a false statement, half-truth, or innuendos, it does not mean it's a statement of truth. Jesus is the Truth (John 14:6, John 17:17, John 1:1). The Holy Spirit is the Spirit of Truth (John 16:13), and He wants us to be set free by the truth (John 8:32). No wonder Prov 23:23 cautioned us not to do away with the truth.

GOD, THE GIVER

Let us look at two statements in the Bible to examine further this issue of knowing God's will. The first one is the one opined by Job, and the second one is the assertion by the Devil when tempting Jesus. Let's look at Job's statement in Job 1:21 - the Lord gives, and the Lord has taken away. Is it true? Is that the description of the nature and character of God? We have to know what God gives and what He does not give. Let's look at some scriptures:

- For God so loved the world that He **gave** His only begotten son – **John 3:16 (KJV)**
- Yea, the Lord shall **give** that which is good; and our land shall yield her increase – **Ps 85:12 (KJV)**
- The Lord will **give** grace and glory; no good thing will He withhold from them that walk uprightly –**Ps 84:11 (KJV)**
- Delight yourself in the Lord; And He will **give** you the desires of your heart – **Ps 37:4 (NASB)**
- Now the Lord of peace Himself **give** you peace always by all means – **2 Thess 3:16 (KJV)**
- I am the Lord your God…to **give** you the land of Canaan, and to be your God – **Lev 25:38 (KJV)**
- Since He did not spare even His own Son but gave Him up for us all, won't He also **give** us everything else? – **Rom 8:32 (NLT)**
- For His divine power has **granted** to us everything pertaining to life and godliness, through the true knowledge of Him who called us by His own glory and excellence. – **2 Peter 1:3 (NASB)**
- For God's gifts and His call can never be withdrawn. – **Rom 11:29 (NLT)**

Now we see from the preceding verses of scripture that God is the one who is always giving, and when He gives, He is not in the habit of taking it back. We have to be careful about assuming some things about God. He is not the one who took away the blessing upon Job's Life; it was the Devil. The Lord was not the one who took his children; it was the Devil. When God takes people, He takes them alive, not dead – Enoch (Gen 5:22-24); Elijah (2 Kings 2:11); Jesus (Acts 1:9-11); The Church (1 Thess 4:16-17).

THE DEATH QUESTION

Well, someone may be wondering if death is not part of life. Yes, death is part of man's lifecycle on earth. Ecc 3:1-2 says: **To everything, there is a season, A time for every purpose under heaven: A time to be born, And a time to die; A time to plant, And a time to pluck what is planted;(NKJV).** From the rudimentary understanding of the indefinite article "a" in the English Language, we know that it modifies non-specific or non-particular nouns. So, a time, a season, etc., all describe indefinite, non-specific events. That is why babies are born at different times and people die at different times. Let us proceed by saying that God is the one who created times and seasons (Gen 1:14), and He also has the sole right to change times and seasons (Dan 2:21).

Knowing God's intention and plan for a man between the cradle (time of birth) and the grave (time of death) is essential. Even though death is part of the equation according to **Heb 9:27: And as it is appointed for men to die once, but after this the judgment (NKJV).** Nevertheless, God wants every man and woman to live a long, fulfilling life. This intention is expressed in **Ps 91:16. With long life, I will satisfy him And show him My salvation (NKJV).**

How do we quantify long life? Is there a specific number that indicates this? God always makes us aware of His thoughts and intentions about many things if only we can seek His knowledge. So, yes, there is a specific number that expresses God's original intention for long life. We see God talking about this in **Gen 6:3: And the Lord said, "My Spirit shall not strive with man forever, for he *is* indeed flesh; yet his days shall be one hundred and twenty years." (NKJV).**

So, between the cradle and the grave, everyone has the potential to live a hundred and twenty (120) years! The Bible also declares in **Ps 61:6, "You will prolong the king's life. His years as many generations."(NKJV).** If this is true, why do people die young and, in some cases, too young? For starters, we need to realize that every man and woman, irrespective of their religious persuasion, have an eternal enemy, the Devil or Satan, whose modus operandi is: To steal, to kill, and destroy (John 10:10). This enemy is the source of all the evil work we see on earth. He influences division, hatred, lies, confusion, ungodliness, murders, disagreement, wars, acts of wickedness, sicknesses, and diseases. The enemy is all out to destroy all that is good.

Also, we must even recognize that our actions or inactions sometimes make us play into the enemy's hand, making him take advantage of people leading to their untimely death. God, in His infinite wisdom, gives us specific things that can shorten people's lives.

God commands us to honor our parents so that we can live long (Exo 20:12, Deut 5:16, Eph 6:2). He also admonishes us to keep His laws, ways, and commandments (Deut 5:33, 1 Kings 3:14, Prov 3:1-2); He wants us to put His rules in our hearts and teach our children (Deut 11:18-21). God delights in our reverence for Him (Prov 9:10-11, Prov 10:27), and He also rewards our service to Him (Exo 23:25-26, Job 36:11). He also does not want us to speak evil or deceitful things (1 Pet 3:10).

In conclusion, we have a part to play in ensuring that God's intention of experiencing a long, prosperous life. We can start by renewing our mindset about things we hear versus what the scriptures say specifically about them. No matter what, God's word should have the ultimate authority over our conduct and life so we can have the necessary ammunition against the enemy's tricks.

DEALING WITH THE LIES OF THE ENEMY

One prominent trick of the enemy is to present half-truths about people, situations, and our future. The pronouncement made by Satan in Luke 4:5-7 about giving Jesus the power is a half-truth, and since Jesus has been resurrected, that statement has become null and void. The Devil got that power through the sell-out of Adam in the garden before Jesus was ever born on earth. God initially gave Adam the leasing right of the earth (Ps 115:16), but when Adam and Eve decided to obey the Devil instead of God, they gave that lease/right to the Devil. All this is still not in the plan and purpose of God for man, so Jesus had to show up to collect back what was originally man's right.

So, after Jesus was resurrected, three specific and dramatic changes occurred.

1. Jesus has all power (Authority) in heaven and on earth (Mat 28:18, Rev 1:8).
2. The Devil is no longer harmed, and he's been stripped of the lease of Adam (Col 2:15; Rev 1:18)
3. Man has regained the authority to rule again (Luke 10:19, Math 16:18-19; I John 4:4, 5:4).

We must understand the dispensations of God's mandate for man. The revelations of the Holy Scriptures should progressively unveil our knowledge about His purpose and human destiny. So, the responsibility is on us to know what God is saying and appropriate what belongs to us. We shouldn't accept just anything as God's will for our lives. No matter how well-meaning someone tries to convey things to us, that is somewhat contrary to God's original intention for our lives. We've sometimes heard and come across some of those religious talks:

"God is surely teaching me some things through this sickness." No, God is not the author of sickness, and He is always in the business of healing (Ps 107:20, Exo 23:25)

"Well, you know God is not giving us much so that we may remain humble." No, God always gives us more than enough because He is El-Shaddai (Ps 23:1, Ps 36:9, John 10:10).

"You know Jesus said it is easier for a camel to pass through the eye of the needle than for a rich man to get to heaven." Jesus was referring to those who trust in their riches rather than God. (Gen 13:2, Prov 10:22, Job 36:11)

"If it's God's will, then He will just do anything He wants to do." Again, No, God always works with our cooperation in any situation we find ourselves in (Mat 7:7).

"I don't want any of this world's goods, heaven is my home, and I'm just passing through this world." Ultimately, even after this earth is destroyed, there will still be another new one. The earth is made specifically for man to inhabit (Ps 115:16, Isa 66:22, 2 Pet 3:13, Rev 21:1)

"He was such a nice young man, but it's a pity he died young. Well, the Lord gives, and the Lord takes away." God plans that we live long and fulfill our destiny. (Exo 23:26, Ps 91:16)

I could go on and on about some of the conversations we encounter daily in the lives of believers. During my college days, I knew of someone that had Sickle Cell Anemia. While going through these attacks, he missed semester exams because he would have to be taken home for appropriate care. You could imagine what was happening to his GPA and class attendance. It was a recurring challenge for him until he finally took a stand on God's promises in the Bible about Jesus healing him some 2000 years ago. He finally got healed of the terrible condition.

The Bible teacher, Joyce Meyer, also had her battle with Cancer, but she addressed it immediately by declaring healing scriptures over her body. Later, when she went for the tests, the Doctors saw that the Cancer cells had been burnt by fire. She's been living free from Cancer ever since.

During Kenneth Copeland Southwest Believers Convention, a Lady Minister testified to being diagnosed with Cancer and later healed. After she got all the doctors' results confirming her condition, she went home sad, which weighed heavily on her emotions. However, her dad helped her get back on track by prodding her that if indeed she is a Minister of the Gospel, it must be proved. He said to her daughter, "physician heal thyself." At this realization, she decided to gather all the scriptures about healing. She began to study, pray, and confess them for the remaining thirty days she's been given.

On the 28th day, she went in for her scheduled appointment, and something dramatic occurred. After the doctors examined her, she was asked to wait in the lobby while collating the results. While waiting, unknown to her, the doctors discussed the test results among themselves and glanced at her occasionally. They just could not believe what they were seeing. The test results showed no trace of Cancer, which was an outstanding miracle. So, they gave her a medical certificate stating that she once had Cancer and now is entirely free from it. Hallelujah! Things don't change for the better until we come to grips with God's will for our situation. We must endeavor to always be in the know regarding God's will.

DIMENSIONS OF GOD'S WILL

The Apostle Paul made us aware of the three aspects of God's will in Romans 12:2:

> *And do not be conformed to this world, but be transformed by the renewing of your mind, that you*

may prove what is that good and acceptable and perfect will of God (NKJV).

So, we see a progression of God's will's acceptable, good, and perfect domain. Even though these three dimensions are embedded, God's best is still the perfect will. We will look at these three briefly.

God's Perfect will

This dimension of God's will represents God's original intention or plan. It symbolizes His absolute truth or reality as expressed in salvation, healing, blessing, forgiveness, marriage, etc. We see this in Abraham's Life when God promised him that he would be a father of nations and that Sarah, his wife, would bear him a male child (Gen 17, 18). It looked impossible from all physical standpoints, yet God fulfilled it, and Sarah gave birth to Isaac (Gen 21:1-3).

Another classic example is God's intention to deliver the children of Israel from the bondage of Egypt and take them to a good land flowing with milk and honey. In the New Testament, the ready example is God's plan for Jesus to redeem fallen man from sin and death (Mat 1:21, Gal 1:4, Col 1:13-14, John 3:16, Gal 3:13-14). The book of Acts 4:12 epitomized God's plan of salvation, declaring that:

Nor is there salvation in any other, for there is no other name under heaven given among men by which we must be saved (NKJV).

God also made known the procedure for this salvation as Apostle Paul reveals in Rom 10:9-10:

that if you confess with your mouth, the Lord Jesus and believe in your heart that God has raised Him from the dead, you will be saved. For with the heart,

one believes unto righteousness, and with the
mouth, confession is made unto salvation (NKJV).

There is no ambiguity about God's plan, purpose, and intention in all these three examples of His perfect will. They all had nothing to do with how a man feels or thinks about the idea. The power and the host of heaven divinely back it up. There is always angelic support and assistance for the perfect will of God (Ps 103:19). We saw that in the fulfillment of those three examples.

Just four years ago, at 25 weeks of pregnancy, Chine Chike's wife was diagnosed with severe preeclampsia with extremely high blood pressure. The news was disheartening to the family, and the outlook was bleak. The doctors suggested that the baby could have died, and they were preparing for an emergency hysterectomy to remove the wife's uterus. At this point, Chine began to pray to God, with whom nothing is impossible. He finally got a Yes! Also, he got the miracle of a lifetime. The doctors canceled the surgery, the wife survived, and their baby was delivered at 26th weeks, hale and healthy to the glory of God.

God's Good Will

In this second dimension of God's will, we see the impact of men's decisions to act in resonance with an attribute or character of God. It might not be expressed fully as the perfect will of God, but there is a resemblance. Due to this similarity, even when a man originates it, God always recognizes it and releases his divine blessing on it.

Abimelech was a king who took Sarah because Abraham lied to him that she was his sister (Gen 20:1-14). God originally intended to kill the king but could not because Abimelech said he did not sleep with Sarah because of his heart's integrity. God accepted his decision to act honorable and overturned His planned judgment.

Similarly, we also see the trend in King David's life, who had many opportunities to harm the reigning King Saul but decided not to do it. Maybe he had a nudge telling him that vengeance belongs to the Lord. Joseph was another individual who chose not to sleep with his master's wife (Gen 39:7-20). There is also the duo of Joshua and Caleb, who were courageous enough to dare to stick their necks out to boldly declare that they were well able to possess the land they went out to spy (Numbers 13:30). We see God showing up to reward these right decisions and giving His divine approval and backing in all these decisions.

God's Permissive Will

The permissive will is like the good will in that they are both based on human decisions. One is patterned after God's nature and enjoys divine approval, support, and resources, while the other is quite the opposite. The permissive will entails man making decisions most likely contrary to God's plan, intention, or purposes. A perfect example of this narrative is Sarah suggesting that Abraham take Hagar and try to have a baby with her (Gen 16) when God had explicitly told Abraham that Sarah would bear a child (Gen 15). The world is still reeling from that decision with the creation of two often-conflicting nations. On the one hand, the descendants of Isaac (Jews-Israel), and on the second, those of Ishmael (Arabs-Islam). These two nations continually claim ancestral rights to their Palestine land, often resulting in war.

There is always a repercussion and a price to pay when we make decisions contrary to God's expected outcomes. Look at the story of the Israelites in the wilderness. Out of all the people that left Egypt, only two (Joshua and Caleb) of that generation entered the promised land (Num 14). God does not take His purpose lightly, and although He might allow our decisions to prevail due to ego, pride, and self-will, there are always unsavory consequences. No wonder one of the crucial prayers of the Apostle Paul was to be filled with the spirit of wisdom and revelation in the knowledge of His will that the eyes of our understanding may be enlightened (Eph 1:17)

WHAT IS UNDERSTANDING?

While we can ascertain God's will through knowledge, it takes understanding to navigate the subject's what, who, why, and when aspects. It's like when the Apostle Paul talked about comprehending the breadth, length, depth, and height of God's love (Eph 3:8). We all know that knowledge simply means the collection of tangible facts about a subject matter. That is what the library or collections of reading materials consist of. It's about the body of knowledge.

On the other hand, wisdom is applying those facts to proffer solutions or answers to problems. However, understanding is not on the same level as knowledge because it seems beyond human reasoning faculties' limits. It sometimes bypasses the realm of the known into the unknown. Let's look at the Vine's Expository Dictionary for some Greek words that provide insight into what it means to [1] understand:

1. NOEO – To perceive with the mind, not with feeling. Rom 1:20, John 12:40
2. SUNESIS – To bring or set together. A sort of amalgamation of diverse sources of knowledge. It means the ability to recognize patterns or intelligence (Mark 12:33); it also means reflective thought (Luke 2:7)
3. GINOSKO – To know or to come to know in full (Acts 8:30, John 8:27, 43; Mat 26:10-13)

While other words in the Greek language further explain what understanding connotes, I just want to limit this discussion to those three words. So, we can have a pseudo definition of understanding as something we can only perceive fully with the mind. This explanation is similar to a large aggregation of knowledge.

In the account of Jesus in Matthew 26:10, there was one interesting fact about understanding. A woman came to pour Alabaster oil on Jesus, and He couldn't immediately pinpoint why this was happening. Nevertheless, Jesus got up to speed with what was happening, and the story continued like this: **When Jesus understood it, he said unto them, Why trouble ye the woman? for she hath wrought a good work upon me (KJV).**

Yes, Jesus did not know what was happening initially, but He got the gist later. Even though everyone knew what the woman was doing, no one understood its divine purpose. There was a time lag until the understanding came to Jesus about the divine plan. I want to say this about this subject; understanding is not something we potentially possess. It comes upon an individual. It comes just like when we get inspiration for a song or other similar unique experiences. I believe this is the apt description of Job 32:8: **But there is a Spirit in man, and the breath of the Almighty gives him understanding (NKJV)**

I like to give a little acronym for the meaning of understanding: CID

C – Comprehension

I – Interpretation

D – Discernment

When we understand, we can easily see those three elements of comprehension, interpretation, and discernment. These three do work together.

THE SOURCES OF UNDERSTANDING

Yes, man has the unique ability to understand many things. However, we must remember that he is still limited compared to God, the creator of all things, whose understanding is infinite (Ps

147:5). It is interesting to know where understanding stems from and how we can access these sources.

1. God, the Father

From the scriptures, we realize that God Almighty is a giver of understanding. Prov 2:6 says, **"For the Lord gives wisdom; From His mouth come knowledge and understanding (NKJV)."** Again, Prov 9:10 also tells us that **"The fear of the Lord is the beginning of wisdom, And the knowledge of the Holy One is understanding (NKJV)."** We see that God is the primary source of understanding, and the more we know and interact with Him, the more we are impacted by the spirit of understanding. It is not surprising that when King Solomon had an opportunity to ask anything from God, an open cheque, he only requested an understanding heart (1 Kings 3:9, 4:29). We also see God announcing to Moses in Exodus 31:1-3 that He has given Bezaleel understanding, wisdom, and knowledge. All these should encourage the believer to approach God and ask for an understanding heart, and God will readily oblige to the request.

2. Jesus Christ

it is expected that the Son of God will manifest the same qualities expressed by God the Father. For this reason, Jesus was able to impact the disciples with understanding in Luke 24:45 when it says, **"then opened He their understanding, that they might understand the scriptures (KJV).** The Apostle John also elucidates this point in 1 John 5:20:

> *And we know that the Son of God has come and has given us an understanding, that we may know Him who is true; and we are in Him who is true, in His Son Jesus Christ. This is the true God and eternal life (NKJV)*

3. Holy Spirit

In chapter 2, we talked about the primary purpose of the Holy Spirit. We now consider another aspect of His ministry. We must realize that there is understanding, and then there is a spirit of understanding. Just like there is faith and then the spirit of faith. Also, there is truth and then the spirit of truth. So, no matter the subject we are dealing with, it could exist in one dimension and multiple dimensions: the spirit or the fullness of that particular expression. Job 32:8 says, **"There is a spirit in man, and the breath (Holy Spirit) of the Almighty gives them understanding." (KJV)** This spiritual impartation could mean a one-time, one-off, or as-needed basis. On the contrary, the account of the Prophet Isaiah in Isa 11:2-3 says:

The Spirit of the Lord shall rest upon Him,
The spirit of wisdom and understanding,
The spirit of counsel and might,
The spirit of knowledge and the fear of the Lord. (KJV)

This endowment indicates something different, something more permanent, far-reaching, and more imparting. This is the fundamental reason the Apostle Paul was so particular that the believers at Ephesus should be filled with the spirit of wisdom and revelation (Understanding). Eph 1:17

"I ask the glorious Father and God of our Lord Jesus Christ to give you his spirit. The spirit will make you wise and let you understand what it means to know God (CEV)."

4. Word of God

The Lord Jesus Christ emphatically told us that the words He speaks are spirit and carry life (John 6:63). Consequently, the word of God brings the same life and attributes of God. Therefore, whenever the word of God is released through teaching and preaching, it usually

81

impacts understanding, according to Ps 119:130. "**The unfolding of your words gives light; it imparts understanding to the simple (ESV).** Another way that we get impacted with understanding is when we meditate in God's word (Ps 119:99-100)

5. Ministry Gifts

In God's wisdom, He delegates His ministers as a conduit of His ability to impact believers with understanding. Jer 3:15 says:

"And I will give you shepherds after my own heart, who will feed you with knowledge and understanding (ESV).

The shepherd could be a Pastor, a bible class teacher, a Sunday school teacher, Apostle, Teacher, Evangelist, or anyone called and anointed to ministry.

Through the supernatural gift of Prophecy in the Holy Spirit, people often get a sense of understanding. The Apostle Paul said in 1 Corinthians 12:10:

> *To another the working of miracles, to another prophetic insight (the gift of interpreting the divine will and purpose); to another the ability to discern and distinguish between [the utterances of true] spirits [and false ones], to another various kinds of [unknown] tongues, to another the ability to interpret [such] tongues. (AMPC)*

6. Issachar Anointing

For the church, the body of Christ, to fulfill the great commission mandated in Matt 28, people need to be involved. Jesus said we should pray for laborers. I think those laborers would be operating in the Issachar Anointing (I Chronicles 12:32), which typically models a group of people with the ability to understand the different seasons of God's plan, purpose, and kingdom agenda.

KEYS TO UNDERSTANDING

Some specific keys in the kingdom of God are available to the child of God. These keys aid us in understanding our covenant rights and privileges better. The two primary keys are (1) the validity of the word of God (2 Tim 2:15), (2) the reality of the Holy Spirit (I John 2:27). Words in their native state are the most potent force on earth as explained in these scriptures John 1:1-3, Col 1:16, Ps 33:6, Ps 119:6, Heb 1:1, Heb 11:1-3. I concurred with Rev Funke Adejumo's assertion that "life is not governed by miracles but by the understanding of God's eternal principles in His word."

It is also essential to realize the nature and the three dimensions of God's word (Logos, Rhema, Living person). Finally, words are an image-transferring device; hence we create things by speaking them out. I would discuss this in chapter 5, which deals with the conditions that must be met for prayers to be answered.

Why Understanding?

At this point in the discussion, some might be asking what has understanding got to do with praying to God. At least God loves us, and He has given us all things to enjoy. Please note that no matter how wise a person thinks he is, they still need understanding (Prov 4:7). Wisdom works in conjunction with understanding.

The primary reason we need understanding is to manifest our sonship in Christ (Rom 8:19). We all have a prophetic mandate to be the salt of the earth and shine in this world as a city set upon a hill (Mat 5:13-16), but it requires an inward light first (Isa 60:1-3, 2 Pet 1:19). Until we have the light of God (understanding), first, we cannot fully grasp the many things He has freely given us. Until a cellphone syncs up with a cell tower, there is bound to be a signal loss.

CHAPTER 4

CONNECTIVITY IN PRAYER

We can view Prayer as an event in the time sequence of experiences or the lifecycle of things. It is also perceived as an act of communication, which is the bedrock of any relationship model: husband-wife, parent-child; leader-follower; boss-subordinates; manager-staff, etc. Prayer is similar to a circle or chain held together without any missing link or separation. The Rev. George Adegboye once commented, " Prayer is a planned outcome of an ongoing dialogue." God designed the human world to be in continuous communication with the Man and Woman He created. He visits Man to have dialogue, knowledge, awareness, and care. In Gen 3:8, we see God in one of those times:

And they heard the sound of the Lord God walking in the garden in the cool of the day, and Adam and his wife hid themselves from the presence of the Lord God among the trees of the garden. (NKJV)

God's original intention is to become intimate with His creation, not just to be a prayer-answering God. In his book, *Praying with Power*, Peter Wagner commented, " The essence of prayer is a personal relationship between a believer and God." However, we see a contradiction with Adam and Eve leaving the garden of Eden, which God initially prepared for them. That regrettable action began the painful spiritual distancing between God and Mankind. In the typical electronic communication system model, connectivity means no signal loss. In the Old Testament, we observe that when a man does not know God or has any dealings with Him, his prayers seem not to be answered. David said in Ps 66:12

If I regard iniquity in my heart, The Lord will not hear (NKJV). Equally, in Isa 59:1-3, the scriptures say:

> *Behold, the Lord's hand is not shortened, That it cannot save; Nor His ear heavy,*
>
> *That it cannot hear. But your iniquities have separated you from your God; And your sins have hidden His face from you, So that He will not hear. For your hands are defiled with [a]blood, And your fingers with iniquity; Your lips have spoken lies, Your tongue has muttered perversity (NKJV).*

We can note that God is ever willing to answer Prayer, but where there are iniquity, sin, and transgressions, He does not seem obliged to grant such a request. After King Solomon completed building the Lord's temple and was dedicating it, he asked God to fulfill his promises to Israel. However, God appeared to him in the night and gave him His principles in 2 Chronicles 7:13-15:

> *When I shut up heaven, and there is no rain, or command the locusts to devour the land, or send pestilence among My people, if My people who are called by My name will humble themselves, and pray and seek My face, and turn from their wicked*

ways, then I will hear from heaven and will forgive their sin and heal their land. Now My eyes will be open, and My ears attentive to prayer made in this place. (NKJV)

Tellingly, whenever the children of Israel failed to do what was right, God didn't hear their prayers until they repented. Dr. Leroy Thompson sum it up, "God's principle supersedes prayer, and prayer won't work against principles."

REPENTANCE

One fundamental principle God instituted into His relationship with Man is repentance (Heb 6:1). We see the trail of repentance from the Old Testament into the New Testament. God's desire for men and women is for them to repent from evil, sin, and iniquity. The act of repentance involves a change of mindset, thought patterns, attitude, and actions. Isa 55:7 says: **Let the wicked forsake his way, And the unrighteous man his thoughts; Let him return to the Lord, And He will have mercy on him; And to our God, For He will abundantly pardon. (NKJV).**

Repentance repairs the broken piece in the relationship between God and Man. It is the process whereby we can get right with God (2 Chron 7:14). Repentance is the basis of the mission and purpose of Jesus Christ (Mark 2:17; Luke 5:32; Luke 24:47; Acts 5:31; Eze 14:6). By creative covenant rights, God is compelled to hear every Prayer made by any man or woman (Ps 65:2), whether by a sinner or righteous person. However, God is not under compulsion to answer every Prayer He hears.

It is our Prayer that determines the kind of Prayer outcome we get. If there is a blockage in the connectivity pipeline, answers to Prayer would be delayed or denied. This unintended outcome is due to the law of cause and effect, as expressed in Gen 8:22, Gal 6:7. Hence whatever is sown will be reaped, good or bad.

Templately, the law of cause and effect was the determining factor in answering prayers during the Old Testament. This ideology is the basis for answers to prayers during that dispensation. In Gen 20, king Abimelech did not die even after God pronounced judgment. He was able to escape that intended judgment based on the integrity of his heart (Gen 20:5). In the same light, we also see in Isa 38 that king Hezekiah prayed to God to avert another similar judgment of death. He was able to reverse the pronouncement by pleading that he had sowed good deeds in time past. This reason was enough evidence that God added fifteen more years to his life (Isa 38:1-5). I believe this is the situation that David referred to in Ps 20:1-4.

> *May the Lord answer you in the day of trouble; May the name of the God of Jacob defend you; May He send you help from the sanctuary, And strengthen you out of Zion; May He remember all your offerings, And accept your burnt sacrifice. Selah. May He grant you according to your heart's desire And fulfill all your purpose. (NKJV).*

ABIDE IN ME

While the standard practice during the Old Testament era was for people to be judged based on what they did right or wrong in God's sight. The outcome of such an appraisal determines whether there would be answers to the Prayer made. However, in the New Testament, we see Jesus showing us a more excellent way of getting a Yes! To our prayers. In John 15:7-8, Jesus said:

If you remain in me and my words remain in you, ask whatever you wish, and it will be done for you. This is to my Father's glory, that you bear much fruit, showing yourselves to be my disciples. (NIV).

From the preceding statement, we know Jesus enumerated four essential things:

1. Remain in me (Jesus) – **Connectivity of Prayer.**
2. Let God's word remain in you – **Conditionality of Prayer**
3. You will have whatever you ask – **Covenant of Prayer**
4. God is glorified when there are answers to prayers – **Victory of Prayer**

We will only look at Prayer's connectivity in this chapter and deal with the others in subsequent chapters. Let's look at the shades of meaning of what Jesus was trying to explain in those scriptural verses. The word "abide" means to stay, remain, continue, and connect. It means to be God-inside-mindedness or conscious. To abide in Christ would also connote that we are dwelling in Him. No wonder David said in Ps 91:1 **He who dwells in the secret place of the Most High Shall abide under the shadow of the Almighty**. It's a no-brainer that the Apostle Paul will also echo this when he said, **"For in him we live, and move and have our being"** (Acts 17:28 (NKJV).

I experienced this total dependency on God in the summer of 2017; during my Doctorate program, the committee chair decided I needed a significant redaction of my dissertation papers. Initially, there was a debate about the theoretical/conceptual framework for the research. This update would substantially change the literature review, methodology, results, etc. The academic liaison set the proposed graduating date for the spring of 2018. The situation was not looking pretty, and there was not enough time to get all this extra work done, with all the other things needing my attention. It is one thing if you know exactly where to go digging for specific answers and quite the opposite if you are at a loss. I was in a later state of confusion and disbelief at the possibility of not finishing my program on time. I knew the only solace was in God, so I asked the Lord in Prayer about the right way to get through this maze. After that, I started understanding the perfect theoretical framework I could use to validate my research. It was like a rolling stone, and the needed literature, discussions, and research data started taking shape, and I was inspired to complete the dissertation a month before the deadline.

We need to realize the uniqueness of this connectivity with God. In our modern, technologically wired world, we can quickly identify this process in the cellular communications network model, where our mobile device connects to a cell tower. As long as we have some connectivity to that cell tower, as indicated by the number of signal bars on our device, we are confident that we can receive or make a call. However, in a situation where we are in a remote area with little or no signal connectivity, we find it extremely difficult to make or receive calls.

In this analogy, our phone represents the believer; the signal represents the connection (abide); the actual call is the prayer details, and the cell tower represents the Holy Spirit (John 14:16; 16:13-15).

Yes, we connect through the Holy Spirit's function because Jesus said the Holy Spirit would remain with us forever (John 14:16-17). Dr. Lester Sumrall said, "It is the Holy Spirit who moves back and forth, bringing communication from our hearts to God and from God's heart to us." When Jesus connects with us, we can feel His pulse and help stir our desires. This unique connectivity helps us to discern the Father's will even before we make such prayers. We have advanced knowledge of what God will entertain or will not allow; hence we are usually on the same page and understanding with God.

There was a time when Pastor John Hagee's mother was diagnosed with colon cancer. The doctor's prognosis was heart-wrenching with the expected chemotherapy weeks, followed by a colostomy surgery. Even with all these, it seems it's going to be terminal, and death will be the end of it. The Hagee family gathered to pray for this woman of God, pressing into the promises of Ps 91 and taking a stand that God will fulfill His word and heal her. Their prayers got a Yes! First, the radiation didn't affect her skin as they had expected, and then the period for the surgery was cut short because the doctors didn't have to perform the colostomy. When they open her up, the size of the tumor had reduced significantly, and they were able to cut it all out.

Connectivity is one of the most significant issues relating to God that marked Jesus's earthly ministry. John 8:29 declares: **And He who sent Me is with Me. The Father has not left Me alone, for I always do those things that please Him (NKJV).**

How to Connect

The obvious question in our hearts is, "how can one connect with God and maintain such a state?" There are three primary ways believers can exercise and practice their connectivity with God. The first way is simply through acknowledgment, while the second method is by recognition, and the last is when we praise and worship God. We will look at these three now to seek understanding.

1. Acknowledgment

This entails an understanding to accept the existence of someone. For instance, during a wedding ceremony, there is a lot of waiting and anxiety about when the bride will make her grand entrance. Even though she comes in later, the event will only proceed with her presence. Sometimes she came later than scheduled, but we all, along with the anxious groom, had to endure and wait for the bride to show up. And when the bride finally shows up, we dare not be found sitting down! Some might dare, but cumulative embarrassment from many eyes will be too much to bear. So, in wisdom, it is appropriate just to stand and acknowledge, here comes the bride! In like manner, God wants us to recognize Him. I love the book by Pastor Benny Hinn titled: *Good Morning, Holy Spirit.* The book depicts the type of conversation attitude we can develop in our communion with the Holy Spirit.

To acknowledge God's presence is to recognize that He is always there with us right now. Heb 11:6 declares that: **But without faith, it is impossible to please Him, for he who comes to God must believe that He is and that He is a rewarder of those who diligently seek Him (NKJV).**

The word of God must fully persuade us that God is with us even when our natural inclination might present a false reality. We must persist in catching a glimpse of His person as seeing into the realm of the invisible (Heb 11:27).

2. Recognition

The next consequential thing that follows our act of acknowledging God is recognizing His supreme, infinite abilities. It is in knowing that **"Now to him who is able to do immeasurably more than all we ask or imagine, according to his power that is at work within us" (Eph 3:20, NKJV).** The elements of recognition entail giving up the driver's seat of our lives. It allows our circumstances (salvation, sickness, deliverance, safety, provision, burden, poverty) to become swapped with God's abilities.

We must endure seeing God in our prayers and with our prayers rather than the issue or the situation. Whatever we dwell or focus on expands exponentially.

Before we even begin to bombard heaven with prayer requests, the principal purpose of connecting with God is to know that the

Prayer will be answered. Some time ago, back in Nigeria, I boarded a public vehicle. As the bus was about to move, I could hear the Devil whisper in my ears about the possibility of a car accident. But then I remembered the scriptures He will never leave nor forsake me, and if God is true to me, then I need to recognize Him and then see whether the intended accident will take God out. After this mindset, I started praying in the spirit (tongues) to validate my scriptural understanding of God's presence. At the end of the journey, there was no accident or incident throughout the whole trip.

By acknowledging and recognizing His divine ability, we are automatically set to understand His mindset (1 Cor 2:16). This expectation is similar to observing protocols during a meeting with a plan. We can predict the outcome of such a gathering by glancing at the discussion points list. Therefore, the connectivity element gives us an immediate acknowledgment flag if there would be answers to the Prayer. Hence, we should not expect uncertainty; instead, we should have exuberant confidence according to 1 John 5:14: **Now this is the confidence that we have in Him, that if we ask anything according to His will, He hears us (NKJV).**

3. Praise is What We Do

The offer of praise and worship is the third aspect of connecting with God after recognizing and acknowledging Him. The surest and best way to fully experience His presence is to enter His gates with thanksgiving and into His courts with praise and worship. It is in this atmosphere of praise and worship that we can sense the divine presence of God. In his teaching on the "Power of Worship," Bishop Don Meares opined that God primarily reveals Himself more in our worship.

We praise Him for what He has done and worship Him for who he is. David said in Ps 22:3 that **"You sit as the Holy One. The praises of Israel are your throne." (NCV).** The old KJV says God

Inhabits the praise of his people, Then, as we praise Him, He starts to inhabit or sit upon our praise, and if the Lord is present in a situation, there will be a turnaround. There is no more effective method for God's manifest presence than when we engage in praise and worship. Ps 50:23 says: **"Whoever offers praise glorifies Me; And to him who orders his conduct aright I will show the salvation of God." (NKJV)**

I remember one time when I applied for a new job. I had completed the testing and all the necessary interview process, but there was a delay in getting an offer. Although the company initially gave me an offer, I made a counteroffer, and I was told they'd need the approval of someone higher up to move forward with me. I remember sitting in the car, and I was like, "ok, Lord, what else am I supposed to be doing now?" Then I felt the Lord nudging me to take a stand and praise Him. So, I started praising Him and worshiping Him even when my mind didn't want to tag along, but I did it anyway. The company later called me to give me the same offer I'd requested. Praise the Lord!

The simple act of praise and worship connects us to the whole universe's power source. This action brings the God of the universe to the scene. In that atmosphere, anything and all things are possible. Bishop David Oyedepo once said, "Praise is what keeps the heavens open; it keeps the rains coming. The Apostle Paul states in Hebrews 13:15**: "Therefore by Him let us continually offer the sacrifice of praise to God, that is, the fruit of our lips, giving thanks to His name." (NKJV)**

Prayer's dialogic nature makes connectivity a fundamental requirement for getting answers to our prayers. We have to be connected to God relationally. When we deliberately do this, we begin to grasp some fundamental principles and rules of engagement to get a Yes from God!

CHAPTER 5

CONDITIONS FOR ANSWERED PRAYER

Whenever we engage God on any level, there are always rules and principles that are at work for a positive outcome. We would be looking at the second most crucial reality of what Jesus said in the classical text we are considering in John 15:7-8:

> *If you remain in me and my words remain in you, ask whatever you wish, and it will be done for you. This is to my Father's glory, that you bear much fruit, showing yourselves to be my disciples. (NIV).*

Here, we get the gist of the statement if my Words remain (Abide) in you. The Lord Jesus Christ said," My Words," not cute quotable quotes, aphorisms, innuendos, anecdotes, or wise sayings. With due respect to the art of communication, I believe there is a place for all these communication fillers and other essential elements of communication; nevertheless, that is not what we need when trying to "Get a Yes" answer from the almighty God.

THE RHEMA WORD

We must try to understand what Jesus was demanding from us here. He is not saying just read the Holy Bible from the book of Genesis to that Revelation's last chapter. Yes, we need the bible knowledge to have a contextual mental frame of reference that's much deeper than that. The word of God exists in three primary forms. There is the Logos form, the Rhema, and the Living Word.

The Logos is the written word of God (Heb 4:12); it is like the alphabet of the English language. It forms the essential building elements of communication in that language. It is from the alphabet that we form words, then sentences, and then paragraphs. That is why God advised us always to get acquitted with it (Prov 4:20). God's words form the basic building block of our divine communication system.

On the other second dimension, the Rhema is the Logos transformed by the Holy Spirit. The specific, inspired Word of God is spoken to a particular individual in a specific situation. In Gen 12:1-4, God tells Abraham to leave his Father's house to a land He will show him. That was a Rhema word spoken to Abraham, and we see through the Holy Bible that God usually gives Rhema to people in a specific unique situation.

We understand the classic story of God delivering the children of Israel in Exodus 14 when they had their backs to the wall and didn't know what to do or where to turn. The Egyptians were on their heels, the red sea was spread out before them, and the Israelites were in a tight corner. However, we see God speaking a Rhema Word to Moses to stretch his rod over the red sea. The sea later patted for them, and they walked on dry ground.

The tremendous power of the Spoken Rhema Word is evident during the creation story in Genesis 1. We see God commanding things into existence, and no contrary force or being could say otherwise. The Rhema word of God is the Logos word that has been empowered or activated by the Holy Spirit. It is a word or statement that the Holy Spirit has breathed upon. Hence it acts as a spiritual sword or weapon. When God tells you something, you can always take it to the bank because it will surely come to pass. Isa 55:10-11 says,

> *For as the rain comes down, and the snow from heaven, And do not return there, But water the earth, And make it bring forth and bud, That it may give seed to the sower and bread to the eater, So shall My word be that goes forth from My mouth; It shall not return to Me void, but it shall accomplish what I please, And it shall prosper in the thing for which I sent it (NKJV).*

Jesus revealed to us that the Rhema word is Spirit and life (John 6:63). It is the word that sustains life and the systems in the universe (Heb 1:3). Just think about that the next time it seems all hope is lost. God can give anyone the greatest supernatural or divine power in any situation, the Rhema Word.

The Rhema Word and all the other forms of the word of God are God himself (John 1:1-4). Lastly, in this understanding of God's word, the third form is the Living Word (Gen 3:8; Rev 19:11-16). This type is the word personified in the Lord Jesus Christ.

We need to genuinely understand what God is saying to us, more so what Jesus meant by "if my words remain in you." Let's look at the various steps that can aid us in unraveling this word of God remaining in us.

Step 1 – Know the Scriptures for yourself.

When we are accustomed to God's stated dealings in the written Holy Bible, we can begin to feel what God feels, think what He thinks, and see the way He sees. Jesus said in John 5:39: **Search the scriptures, for in them you think you have eternal life; and these are they which testify of me (NKJV).** When we dig into the Bible, we become aware of the "who" about God and not necessarily the "what He is." This exercise makes us have revelational knowledge of God that is beyond just memorizing scriptures. This mindset was the innate desire of Apostle Paul, who said in **Phil 3:10: "That I may know him.**"(KJV) This type of knowledge transcends the literal understanding of God and His ways. Instead, it is a kind of experiential learning that comes through a clear path of spiritual discovery. The Lord God emphasized this type of knowledge when He declared in Jer 9:23-24:

> *Thus says the Lord: "Let not the wise man glory in his wisdom, Let not the mighty man glory in his might, Nor let the rich man glory in his riches; But let him who glories glory in this, That he understands and knows Me, That I am the Lord, exercising loving-kindness, judgment, and righteousness in the earth. For in these, I delight,"*
> *says the Lord (NKJV).*

Step 2 – Understand the Scriptures

It is a much-known fact that mere reading or gathering information does not mean there is a comprehension of the subject matter. We remember the Bible talked about the Ethiopian Eunuch reading the Holy Scriptures but had no clue what the words meant until Phillip joined his chariots to explain the particular chapter in the book of Isaiah (Acts 8:30). Does this mean we need a minister to always tell the Bible to us each time we read it? Only in some cases. The fact is that Jesus knew the dilemma we would encounter when trying to know God by just following the teachings of the Bible. That is why He introduced us to the ministry of the Holy Spirit. John 14:26 says",

But the Helper, the Holy Spirit, whom the Father will send in My name, He will teach you all things, and bring to your remembrance all things that I said to you" (NKJV). And again, we see this specific responsibility in John 16:13:

> *However, when He, the Spirit of truth, has come, He will guide you into all truth; for He will not speak on His own authority, but whatever He hears He will speak; and He will tell you things to come (NKJV)*

It takes the Holy Spirit to unravel the scriptures to us (Job 8:32), and give us deep insight into the plan and purpose of God as Apostle Paul wrote in 1 Cor 2:9-10: But as it is written:

> *"Eye has not seen, nor ear heard, Nor have entered into the heart of man the things which God has prepared for those who love Him." But God has revealed them to us through His Spirit. For the Spirit searches all things, yes, the deep things of God. For what Man knows the things of a man except the Spirit of the Man, which is in him? Even so, no one knows the things of God except the Spirit of God. Now we have received, not the Spirit of the world, but the Spirit who is from God, that we might know the things that have been freely given to us by God (NKJV).*

Step 3 – Receive and Accept the Word of God.

It is not the word of God that we read or hear that ultimately makes a difference in our lives or circumstances but rather that particular word of God we receive. Until we know and understand the scriptures, we cannot accept them, and that is why I mentioned those two steps before this third step. In Job 22:22, the Bible says **Receive, please, instruction from His mouth, And lay up His words in your heart (NKJV).** This expectation is the exact thing Jesus said in letting his word remain or abide in us.

I love the testimony of Cleave, one of our musicians at church. Even though he had a job, he wanted something better, and at the same time, he was studying for his master's degree. I encouraged him to continue to apply for opportunities when they show up, irrespective of not completing his Master's. While preaching on a particular Sunday, I moved to where he played the keyboard. I then spoke some prophetic words over him about the next level or something in that direction. At this, all he did was agree and say, "Amen, I received the word." He was later called for an interview, and he accepted the company's job offer.

There is a realization that words are image-transferring or image-carrying devices. Hence, words of fear will transfer fear, while words of encouragement or comfort will create encouragement or comfort. In Mat 13:18, Jesus showed us a correlation between the seed (word) and the soil (heart) in His explanation of the parable of the Sower. The quantity of our word fruit is the amount of the word we hear and keep. This relationship also depends on our ability to recognize the difference between a statement of truth and a truly stated word. We discussed this primary difference earlier in chapter 1.

Step 4 – Speak The Word

The surest way to get the word of God into our hearts is through meditation. It is the process of transferring the Logos into Rhema. It's the secret of success that God told Joshua to observe if he wants to be prosperous continually (Joshua 1:8). Eating raw, uncooked rice would not do our bodies any sound good. Nevertheless, when we apply heat energy, water, vegetables, and condiments to it, we can settle down to a sumptuous meal that would provide nutrients to our bodies. Similarly, the Logos must be cooked through the meditation process to produce Rhema (1 Tim 4:15, 2 Pet 1:19).

The process of meditation involves two elements: Our Thoughts and Our Talk. It requires that we think about what we read, and while thinking, we say or talk (mutter) it back to ourselves. As we begin speaking the word of God, it starts registering in our Spirit Man. In her book, Quantum Faith, Annette Capps made us understand that "Words are energy...the substance from which our world is made is influenced by words." It is this process that Jesus explained in John 6:63: **The words that I speak to you are Spirit, and they are life (NKJV).**

While growing up as a teenager, I used to come down with Malaria Fever now and then. Afterward, my parents will always take me to our family doctor for Malaria injections, and other medication, which usually lasts for a week or so. After listening to the message by Kenneth Hagin titled: *Healing is The Children's Bread*, I was inspired to meditate on some healing scriptures like Mat 8:17 – Himself (Jesus) took our sicknesses and diseases; I Pet 2:24 – by whose stripes you were healed. I started meditating and speaking those scriptures.

The Holy Spirit began to show me the difference between the various past tenses in those scriptures. The word "took" and "were" are both past tenses. As the author of the Bible started to show me all these related scriptures concerning healing, the word began to come alive in my spirit (John 6:63).

Luke 24:32 says: "**And they said to one another, "Did not our heart burn within us while He talked with us on the road, and while He opened the Scriptures to us?"(NKJV).** I started seeing Jesus already with my sickness. The more I visualized this bible verse, the better I felt on the inside.

Even though my physical body was still reeling with the malaria symptoms, I focused my attention on the healing. I later discovered that divine healing is real. It was so real; I could touch it. After that, I prayed the prayer of faith and declared that I was already healed in God's presence, the Father, Son, and the Holy Spirit. Of course, my mind was trying to think differently. I choose not to allow it. Eventually, as I got to school that day, I felt a bolt of warm electricity current surge through me, and I was completely healed. With the Holy Spirit's help, I understood that healing, like many of God's blessings, is already provided for us to accept and appropriate them.

GOD'S PROMISES

Sometimes we can be blindsided by the right word to appropriate. We can eradicate this uncertainty by getting to know God's word that is already given. These words are what we usually call The Promises of God. These promises are already signed, sealed, and delivered into our spiritual mailboxes according to 2 Peter 1:4, **"by which have been given to us exceedingly great and precious promises, that through these you may be partakers of the divine nature, having escaped the corruption that is in the world through lust." (NKJV).**

According to Bible scholars, there are over 8,000 promises of God in the Holy Bible. How many of these do we know and can appropriate for our health, emotions, mind, peace, family, ministry, career, relationships, home, and cities?

For Monisola, a 52-year lady, who had been through many failed relationships with some men, God still made it happen, and He is never late. When God gives you His promise, He is the only one who can bring it to pass.

Monisola met the first man through a singles website after being hesitant. She meets a guy from her area in the country, and things seem to line up well for them. They started exchanging text messages and phone calls within the next couple of months. Then they later met in person, which was love at first sight. Things started happening, and it was a logical conclusion for them to take the next step toward marriage. They set a date for the guy to visit Monisola's parents, but he never showed up. He called some 48 hours before the meeting to request a postponement, which was the last time she heard from him. She tried to contact him through phone and his social media but then discovered she'd been blocked. Monisola became devastated and thought she was cursed because that was her second failed relationship.

How much more can her fragile heart bear? After another 2 years, she met another guy in their church fellowship, and this time around, the man didn't introduce her to his immediate family. Nevertheless, the relationship didn't work out again because he lied to her. He was already married! At this point, Monisola felt like committing suicide because her heart was broken again, and the guy had exploited her finances. She resolved not to get involved with any man again, let alone get married again. She thought she was cursed and didn't understand why she was being jilted repeatedly.

Anyway, she decided to embark on prayer and fasting with her Pastor. God gave her a yes to those prayers she made about her married life, and she later met another man in their church who finally said, "I do," and they are living ever happily together. God has placed a very high premium on His promises as He assured us in **2 Cor 1:20: "For all the promises of God in Him are Yes, and in Him Amen, to the glory of God through us." (NKJV)**

PRAYING FOR THE PROMISES.

No matter the circumstances or Jam, we find ourselves in; the most important thing to God is our knowledge of the particular promise in the Bible that relates to the situation. That is the correct way of approaching the throne of grace. Hosea 14:2 reveals what to do: **"Take with you words, and turn to the Lord: say unto him, Take away all iniquity, and receive us graciously: so will we render the calves of our lips." (KJV).**

God always wants to give us a satisfying glorious life. For Diane Okhiria, that was her experience with her mom, who was diagnosed with ovarian Cancer. At first, when Diane migrated to another country, she had an agreement with God to keep her family safe and healthy. However, she became concerned when she learned of her mother's condition. She cried and prayed that God would honor His covenant promise and make her mom well. After a couple of weeks, the doctors scheduled chemotherapy sessions. While at the first session, the oncology doctor decided to run a new cancer test before proceeding with the treatment. The test came back negative, and God did keep His covenant promise to Diane and gave her a Yes! What an awesome God.

So, no matter the situation, we can evoke God's promises to calm the raging situations. In his book: *Conquering The Spirit of Limitation*, Pastor David Ijeh asserts "God will always give you the best… He will never give you remnants or rejects, so, prepare your mind to fight for it and take absolute possession of it." We are confident in God's promise in **Isaiah 41:10: "Fear not, for I am with you; Be not dismayed, for I am your God. I will strengthen you, Yes, I will help you, I will uphold you with My righteous right hand." (NKJV)**

The early church in Acts of Apostles suffered persecution for their newfound way of Christ-like living. They had healed a man lame from birth at the beautiful gate, and the miracle had generated controversies, and the whole area was in spiritual revival. Many people were in for these astounding divine visitations. Still, the religious leaders saw it as a defiance of their traditions, so the disciples were threatened. In Chapter 4, Peter and John were arrested and then released. Afterward, they gathered fellow believers to pray and quote from Psalms Chapter 2, and they said:

> *"Lord, You are God, who made heaven and earth and the sea, and all that is in them, who by the mouth of Your servant David have said:*

> *'Why did the nations rage, And the people plot vain things? The kings of the earth took their stand, And the rulers were gathered together Against the Lord and against His Christ.'*

> *"For truly against Your holy Servant Jesus, whom You anointed, both Herod and Pontius Pilate, with the Gentiles and the people of Israel, were gathered together to do whatever Your hand and Your purpose determined before to be done. Now, Lord, look on their threats, and grant to Your servants that with all boldness they may speak Your word, by stretching out Your hand to heal, and that signs and wonders may be done through the name of Your holy Servant Jesus." And when they had prayed, the place where they were assembled together was shaken; and they were all filled with the Holy Spirit, and they spoke the word of God with boldness."* (Acts 4:24-31, NKJV).

Let's recap how these first-generation believers got their Yes!

1. They got God's promise specific to their situation.
2. They approached God with these same promises.
3. They then directed God's attention to the similarity between the pledge and their condition.
4. They made a demand on the ability of God to change the situation.
5. They got a resounding Yes!

God's promises should be the main content that overlays our prayers because that is what God primarily looks for in our petitions.

What is written (the Truth) in the Bible is what Jesus upholds before the throne of Grace (Heb 3:1). Someone might be thinking, well, the disciples just quoted David in Psalms 2. Yes, that's right, and if we remember, in earlier chapter 1, I wrote about the differences between a statement of Truth and the Word of Truth. We can see that the characteristics nature of God has been revealed in that particular Psalms of David, so it is a word of Truth.

We also need to realize that some of the words in the book of Psalms are God's prophetic declarations through the Prophetic ministry of David. For instance, we see three subsequent chapters depicting Jesus in three dispensations – Psalms 22 (Jesus on the Earth), Psalms 23 (Jesus's present-day ministry), and Psalms 24 (Jesus second coming).

In the spring of 2004, we got the letter informing us that I had won the Diversity Visa (DV) lottery and, after that, started visa processing the following year. We went for the visa interview, and everything was fine until it was time to issue the visa. We were informed the Homeland office in Washington, DC had an embargo on visa issuance. According to the processing date, even though we were in the month of June, we would need to be in the U.S. before Xmas of 2005. But this embargo of a thing was just not sitting well with me. I was later told that there was a security threat, and the government was trying to respond to it the best way it could. Well, that sounds logical, and what can anyone do except wait? I was just hopeful that the embargo would be lifted.

Almost every day, co-workers, friends, and family members enquire about visas because, according to them, there has been some sad story of people who couldn't get into the country due to expired visas. Well, I do go for morning walks around my office, so this morning, while just prayer-walking, I felt the Holy Spirit stirring within me to pray for the visa, so I started, and before you knew it, the Lord brought up the word in Zech 4:7 **"Who are you, O great mountain? Before Zerubbabel you shall become a plain! And he shall bring forth the capstone With shouts of "Grace, grace to it! (NKJV).** I began saying, "I speak to the Homeland office in Washington,, DC, I take the headstone (the decision-makers), and I cry grace, grace. I speak grace, and I lift up the embargo on the visa. We would not miss our time to departure because God has already said He is taking us into a large place." I prayed earnestly with that Rhema word for some minutes and the burden lifted, and I got a note of victory. Two days later, the consulate called the office asking for me. The lady on the other line said she wanted to inform me that the visas were ready and that we should come to pick up our passports. Praise the Lord!

God is always faithful to give us a Yes! It is essential to know the source of the promise in the Bible we are standing on, but one sure way to know that we are on the right path is when we have the Holy Spirit's help. Like the disciples, who had been filled with the Holy Spirit. I believe He was the one who brought scripture to our remembrance (John16:13).

THE MINISTRY OF THE HOLY SPIRIT AND PRAYERS.

We have mentioned the central role the Holy Spirit plays in the life of a believer. One of the vital keys to getting our prayer requests turned into answers is if they are Holy Spirit inspired or generated. Rom 8:26 declares, **'Likewise the Spirit also helps our weaknesses. For we do not know what we should pray for as we ought, but the Spirit Himself makes intercession for us with groanings which cannot be uttered" (NKJV).**

So, what is that weakness, someone may ask? Well, it means human insufficiency or lack of knowledge about specific details. When we often receive a bad report about a medical condition or the situation of a loved one, our natural mind tends to blank out, and we find out that we cannot articulate our prayer request. In that instance, the Holy Spirit, our comforter, comes to our aid. He simply assesses the situation, and He then gives us insight into the "what" and the "how" to pray.

Some years back, one of my nephews had a convulsion. The parents were not home; it was just the kids, me, and their grandmother who later became hysteric about what was happening to her grandson. I was at a loss about what to do or how I should pray. I remembered, at that point, the Holy Spirit asking me about my nephew's name. I was thinking about his first name, but I didn't see any relevance to what was happening to him. Then, all of a sudden, I remembered his second name, and I believe it's the Holy Spirit trying to make me understand what was happening in direct fulfillment of **Job 32:8 "But there is a spirit in man, And the breath of the Almighty gives him understanding" (NKJV).** My nephew's second name is Ayokunle, which in the Yoruba language means "A House Full of Joy." In the natural, his name contradicts what is happening at that moment.

However, the Holy Spirit then reminded me of the scriptures in Ps 118:15, which says: **The voice of rejoicing and salvation is in the tents of the righteous (NKJV).** Also, the Bible says in I Samuel 25:25: **For as his name is, so is he (NKJV).** The Holy Spirit is an arranger of spiritual realities because He is the Spirit of truth (John 16:13).

Bishop David Ibiyeomie once said that "effective prayers are all about spiritual calculus." So, armed with these fresh insights into what was happening, I started praying in line with the revelation by speaking to the convulsion to stop because my nephew's name is Joy, not sadness or weeping. I declared what the Bible says about the house would be filled with joy. I felt the burden lift, and later, the convulsion stopped. Hallelujah!

There are some things we must understand about prayers that originated from the Holy Spirit. The believers called to be intercessors would realize some of these things; we can share in their experience. Here are some of the typical characteristics associated with the Holy Spirit-inspired prayers:

1. There is a burden

The individual feels a heavy burden that feels like a stomachache or bump. It merely means your spirit man is about to go into spiritual birth. The Bible calls this experience travailing. Apostle Paul mentioned this pattern of Prayer in Galatians 4:19: **My little children, of whom I travail in birth again until Christ be formed in you (KJV).** This inexplicable travailing or groaning is the Holy Spirit enabling you to pray through him.

2. Lack of essential knowledge

You sometimes feel at a loss of not having the full details of what is happening, and most of the time, there's no time to explain. You might not be able to pinpoint what you are praying for, but you just know something is not right. When we are sensitive to the Holy Spirit, He sometimes just gets us to pray with a particular burden for an individual.

Rev. Kenneth Hagin told of a time when his wife couldn't sleep because she had to pray for some of their church members. All she could articulate was that someone's physical life could be in danger. They tried to ascertain who it could be and tried a generic prayer of protection, but the burden won't lift. The prayer burden continued until they agreed that whomever it was that the Lord would reveal the danger to that individual, and then the Prayer burden lifted. Well, God showed the threat to that individual, and the threat was averted. Praise God!

3. Praying more in the Spirit

In Ephesians 6:18, Paul admonished believers to **"And pray with all manner of prayers and supplications in the Spirit."(GNV)** Making the Christian aware that **"he that speaks in an unknown tongue speaks mysteries unto God "(I Cor 14:2, 14-15 NASB).** Praying in the Spirit is the highest form of Prayer. This type of Prayer is devoid of human intentions, formula, or plan; it is originated by God, administered by God, and controlled by Him.

4. Solution-Oriented

One of the promises of God the Father, as expressed in Jer 33:3, is to show us things we don't know when we pray. Praying in the Holy Spirit provides us the unique opportunity to receive images, visions (both open or closed), pictures, and solutions to prayer requests. I remembered praying with some ministers on a 72-hour prayer chain for the Covid19. I had a clear vision of the Lord in a hospital surgical room, flushing out the contaminated blood of individuals. We were praying that God would send the east wind, and I got a burden to pray along that line. I don't know if it was coincident; some days later, I saw someone post a testimony on Facebook that some 7400 patients were discharged from a NY hospital. Alleluia!

5. Declare it

This is a follow-up on the last point. When we do get a vision, dream, picture, or image during praying in the Spirit, we must declare it. The moment we start speaking out the revelation, it forms an overlay over that particular situation. One of the Holy Spirit's primary responsibilities is to reveal spiritual truth or realities (Deut 29:29, 1 Cor 2:9-12). This revealing ministry of the Holy Spirit comes through two processes: a mission to connect to the Holy Spirit's flow. Praying in the Spirit is one of the methods (Jude 20) and then through visions, where the Holy Spirit brings up to speed, bypassing praying time (Amos 3:7). No matter what is revealed, it must be declared for it to be established and manifest in the situation. At this point, let us consider another related condition for answered prayer.

VISION: WHAT DO YOU SEE?

There was a time in the life of the Prophet Jeremiah when God asked him, Jeremiah, what do you see? (Jeremiah 1:11). It is important to note that one of a healthy person's characteristics is the ability to see. It is a known fact of life that we usually go in the direction of our sight. Emphasis exists in the scriptures on getting answers to Prayer through vision. We see that the father of faith, Abraham, was helped to believe that he would become a father of many nations. At first, we see Abraham lamenting to God about being childless (Gen 15:2). However, God

> *brought him outside and said, "look now towards heaven, and count the stars if you are able to number them." And He said to him, so shall your descendants be.' And he believed in the Lord, and*

> *He accounted it to him for righteousness. (Gen*
> *15:5-6) (NKJV).*

God had to make Abraham see something before he could believe it! This requirement is the primary lesson that applies to every man or woman, and we must also see something to achieve something. It's no wonder Prov 29:18 states, **"Where there is no vision, the people perish."(KJV).**

We consider another scenario with Abraham's grandson – Jacob, who desperately needed a change of his dire financial woes. In Gen 31:7-13, we observed God showing Jacob how to mark and differentiate his flock of animals from his father-in-law. By doing this, he experienced compensation with many of the healthier animals, and he became wealthy.

In the book: *To Heal The Sick*, the healing missionary, Frances Hunter, was wondering about the $100,000 cheque someone received. She was concerned that no one had ever given such a large amount to their ministry. The Lord told her that the situation is like that because she had never seen much money coming into their ministry.

Someone might want to interject that maybe God is Partial, and perhaps He makes one rich and the other poor. No, God is never partial (Rom 2:11, Acts 10:34). We are always limited by what we can or cannot see. So, Frances Hunter started asking God for the ability to see people giving into their ministry. She started seeing various amounts of $1,000, $5000, $10,000, etc., and as long as she kept seeing the amount of money, it somehow found its way to their ministry.

At the beginning of this book, I shared my story of losing admission for an academic year due to the verification exercise. My dad agreed that I spend that time in a pre-degree program organized by the University. Upon successfully completing this, students will be allowed to proceed to their choice of study, which is competitive.

I was not bothered by this because I'd decided to sit for the Nigerian University's Joint Admissions & Matriculations Board (JAMB) entrance exam rather than depend on the internal pre-degree program.

Those days, parents and kids take pride in their JAMB admission letters. But then, while mingling with my fellow pre-degree classmates, I will always put up a dress rehearsal for my graduation day with the Bachelors of Engineering (B.Eng) degree's conferment. That was all the academic future I had envisioned. I sat for the JAMB exams while doing the pre-degree stuff.

Some of my classmates would try to remind me that I needed to perform well in the pre-degree program to get into Engineering before I could even start to think about graduating. I realize that faith in God is the path to seeing the result from the beginning. They thought I was daydreaming and somewhat crazy, but I understood the underlying principles. Well, at the end of the pre-degree schooling, I was told I didn't make the mark for the course in Engineering, but they'll admit me for a course in Geology. That news made me feel sad but not too surprised. After that, the JAMB exam results were released, and then different schools started announcing their cut-off mark for admission. The school must accept you before JAMB issues you a letter of admission.

I made the cut-off point for the school I did my pre-college for their Engineering, but because I didn't pick them as my first choice, it was dicey. That means I had to request a change of the first choice. I met one of the school's principal officers about the Geology admission and the desire to change my JAMB school choice. He flatly refused to help me and said I should be satisfied with the course of the program the school gave me. I prayed, then later wrote to the JAMB registrar and the school registrar of my intention to change my first choice of university.

After a couple of weeks, registration exercises had started with the new enrollments, all this while I had collected the registration documents but still needed to submit them. On the last day to submit the registration, I went to the admission board to check the final list of those admitted into the school and went to the Department of Electrical/Electronic Engineering. Right there, I saw I was 7th on that list! The emotions were overwhelming; my academic dream had become a reality. I quickly went to see the principal officer, who told me it was impossible about the news. He was just too surprised but congratulated me that God did a wonder.

It was a manifestation of wonder as I would graduate with a Bachelor of Engineering Degree in Electrical/Electronic Engineering. Our sights often have a great way of shaping and solidify our desires (Ecc 6:9). This attitude was like the Joy that was set before Jesus after He prayed in the garden of Gethsemane (Heb 12:2). The final result of our prayer request does go a long way to determine if we will see it materialize. No wonder Apostle Paul said that **"while we do not look at the things that are seen, but at the things that are not seen. For the things which are seen are temporary, but the things which are not seen are eternal." (NKJV).**

It was the summer of 2014, I had been working for this company for two straight years, and I felt it was time to move on to something else. I had started sending my resume to recruiters and companies and just playing the employment field. So, I was not sure where I would be working or the company. While in the bathroom one evening, I just saw my name on an offer letter on a company letter-headed paper in a flash of vision. I was like, ok, Lord, thank you, and I just received it and praised God for it. That vision gave me a sense of direction, and I knew which company I would work with. After a while, everything happened the way I saw it, and I joined the company. There was no guesswork as the visions came to pass.

All these revelatory answers to situations might seem far-fetched, but it should be something we expect in our daily lives if we are to get a yes! The Bible concludes in Habakkuk 2:3: **This vision is for a future time. It describes the end, and it will be fulfilled. If it seems slow in coming, wait patiently, for it will surely take place. It will not be delayed. (NLT).**

DARE TO BELIEVE

The quintessence of being called a believer is when we believe in God or the unseen possibilities of His inherent nature. We all have an element of believe in ourselves that is devoid of any religious undertone, affinity, or affiliation. It should not come as a surprise that in Heb 11:6, God demanded that: **But without faith, it is impossible to please Him, for he who comes to God MUST BELIEVE that He is and that He is a rewarder of those who diligently seek him (NKJV).**

In its simplicity, belief is the trust or the assurance that we have in something or someone. It is often strapped on the foundation of our conviction, borne out of our conversation. Our belief often hinges on our choice or decision about some things. Once we can make up our minds to be fully persuaded about our options, we are guarded or insulated from unbelief (Heb 3:17-19), doubt, and double-mindedness (James 1:6-8).

We see many desired outcomes in the Bible, where the fundamental requirement is to believe. God's primary gift is salvation through his son – Jesus Christ, yet we cannot receive or experience it without first putting up our belief hats (Acts 16:31, Rom 10:9). We must realize that the Almighty God does not withhold things from us according to the scriptures (Ps 84:11, Rom 8:31-32). Instead, it is our belief that makes things to be the way they are.

We all believe in something (education, family, relationship, career, job) or someone (spouse, boss, parents, teachers, doctors, lawyers). I like to see belief as a digital (yes or no) response or disposition to accept a fact, idea, or person, without doubt, confusion, or reservation.

Thus, this belief we are discussing is part of our God-given right and is often activated by our decision and a choice. I cannot forget the experience of losing my document folder in a taxicab. During the verification exercise of the student's credentials, I took a taxi to campus. I had a traveling bag and the file folder with me when I boarded the cab. However, when I got off, I left the envelope in the vehicle, and I didn't notice until I had gotten to the faculty office where I was to submit the documents. I was astounded at the realization that losing stuff in a public vehicle was a terminal disaster. The hope of recovery was non-existing, and it was scarily impossible. While all these facts were swelling in my head, I made an uncommon decision to believe in the impossible. I accepted the scary fact that I lost the folder and went beyond that to equally take the Scriptural truths that God is everywhere and can do the impossible.

I walked towards the faculty office's open fields and lifted my eyes to heaven, and I just told God that I refused to accept that my folder was entirely missing because I had all my documents in it. I further explained to God that I believed the taxi driver would bring the folder to my faculty office, and I thanked Him for it. Wow! I thought the answer would be quick because my classmates and friends started sharing negative experiences of people who lost stuff in a public vehicle.

I was not perturbed because I had decided to believe in God for the impossible, and I know that the onus rests on me to be steadfast in my conviction. In his book: *Prayer-the neglected Ministry of Jesus*, Pastor Sola Fabunmi said, "To reap the benefits of answered prayer, we must believe what we speak, and we must speak with authority."

Equally, during the waiting period, I'd checked in at the faculty office to see if anyone dropped the folder, and the secretary will always tell me to forget about the bag. My patience was shaky, but I kept my conviction steady and never wavered. Some two weeks after my talk with God, the same secretary telling me to forget about the bag came running to me, telling me that the driver had dropped the folder! Halleluyah! Praise the Lord. God is always a prayer-answering God only if we believe (Mark 9:23). In his book: *The Magic of Thinking Big*, David Schwartz said, "Belief is the thermostat that regulates what we accomplish in life."

I always love the story of the current world's Fastest Man, Usain Bolt, who, before the 2016 Olympics, he started telling people he wanted to be a legend by winning a "triple triple." That is three Olympic Gold medals (100m, 200m, and 4x100m) in three consecutive Olympics (2008, 2012, and 2016). Some people might not agree with the way he talked about this, but I believe he has a strong belief in himself based on a deep conviction. It is somewhat similar to the believer's firm conviction and belief in God's grace and ability.

At the end of the 2016 Olympics, Usain Bolt became a legend by winning three Gold medals in three consecutive games! Our belief drives the fulfillment of our desires, and we cannot believe beyond what we know. That is why it's crucial to have the right kind of knowledge so we can believe right.

I like to submit that God cannot change what we believe; He can only change what we know. We can see this showcased in Abraham's life in Gen 15:5-6 when he had to change what he knew to believe in God for the impossible. This issue of believing is a standard requirement for achieving everything God promised us in His word (Heb 11:6). As long as we abide by the terms of His conditions, we are assured that God will always deliver what He has promised.

ENTER HIS COURTS WITH PRAISE

One thing that I mentioned in the last chapter is about praising God, and I want to reiterate it here as one of the conditions for getting an Answeredd Prayer. The Bible compels us in Ps 100:4: **"Enter into His gates with thanksgiving,** *And* **into His courts with praise. Be thankful to Him,** *and* **bless His name." (KJV).** This illustration concurs with the Prayer model that Jesus taught his disciples to thank and Hallow the name of the Father. Praises, thanksgiving, and worship are strategic methods of getting a unique Yes to our petitions, requests, and desires. We see the account of the Prophet Elisha, who could not give any word of prophecy to the king until a minstrel played (2 Kings 3:14-20).

There was also an account of a host of armies that came against the children of Israel, and Jehoshaphat, the kings, was anxious about a possible defeat. Later on, he was encouraged to seek God and then: "And when he had consulted with the people, he appointed those who should sing to the Lord, and who should praise the beauty of holiness, as they went out before the army and were saying:

> *And when he had consulted with the people, he appointed those who should sing to the Lord, and who should praise the beauty of holiness, as they went out before the army and were saying: "Praise the Lord, For His mercy endures forever." Now when they began to sing and to praise, the Lord set ambushes against the people of Ammon, Moab, and Mount Seir, who had come against Judah; and they were defeated." (2 Chron 20:21-22, NKJV).*

ACTS OF OBEDIENCE

Some things that determine our prayers' outcomes are within our ability. We usually don't have to develop some esoteric supernatural creeds before accomplishing some expertise. I know we've talked about vision and belief along this line, but there is just one more thing to add to this list: our acts of obedience. God chose King Saul in the Bible to lead the people of Israel.

At the onset, he was submissive to the commands and instructions of God. However, there came a period when he was not fully following God's guidance to the letter, which started his downfall because God stopped answering his prayers. The Prophet Samuel told him the reason for this apparent disconnect from God in 1 Sam 15:22: **"But Samuel replied, "What is more pleasing to the Lord: your burnt offerings and sacrifices or your obedience to his voice? Listen! Obedience is better than sacrifice, and submission is better than offering the fat of rams" (NLT)**

One of the surest paths to get answers to our Prayer is when we live a life of obedience to God. Isa 1:19 admonished us that **"If you are willing and obedient, You shall eat the good of the land" (NKJV).** We must realize that there are wonderful riches and beauty when we are open to obey the dictates and promptings of the Lord simply. Those instructions may often not make any natural, logical sense, but the mere fact that it comes from the all-knowing God ought to assure us.

Some of the great things we expect God to accomplish in our lives will not see the light of day until we walk in the path of obedience. Job 36:11 shows us that: **If they obey and serve Him, They shall spend their days in prosperity, and their years in pleasures (KJV).**

A year after I got married, while saving money and planning to move to a better house, the Lord asked us to buy the PA systems for the church we were attending. The amount was almost the equivalent of a two-year lease of the new house we planned to move to. To the natural mind, it was an unreasonable, unrealistic, and unjustified demand on a newly wedded couple.

In my brief dealings with the Lord, I had come to understand that God is truly the only wise God, and if He asks you to do something, there is an eternal reason, so I set out to gather the money by selling my shares and my monthly salary. We bought the equipment and sent it to church, and then I went back to the drawing board to start planning for the new house by Christmas of the following year.

Before all these events, a few years back, God had told me about His plan to relocate me out of my native country, Nigeria. This knowledge informed the decision to adopt "Allan" as my second middle name. Tellingly, a few months after we moved into the new house, as I was preparing to leave for work, the Lord said, "A Large Place, I'm taking you to a Large Place." Later on, we got the letter that we were among those that won the diversity visa (DV) lottery. The day I went to pick up the letter at my Father's house, the Lord said, using Isa 34:17, that He did this for us simply because we obeyed Him when He asked us to buy the PA system. Praise the Lord!

Rev. George Adegboye tells a similar account; while in a church service, God asked him to empty the bulk money he planned to go shopping with rather than the usual offering he wanted to give. He did as God requested with a trembling heart, and then a lady came to that same meeting asking for him. She said God told her to empty her bank account and give the full money (about $22,000) to Rev. George. What a supernatural increase!

God's provisions and answers are sometimes dependent on our acts of obedience. There was a time when Rev. Hagin's sister was sick, and he had prayed all manner of prayers for her to get better, but it seemed it was not working. Then he started making inquiries from the Lord about this. During the dialog, God began to narrate the many times he had told Rev. Hagin to do something or relocate to a particular place he had gladly obeyed. He said that he would heal his sister because of his acts of obedience, and God did exactly that.

We need to develop the capacity to obey God in our everyday experiences. Be it in our calling, assignment, purpose, relationships, and vocation. We do this by following His promptings in our hearts and the expressed commands in the Scriptures. We should remember the words that Mary, the mother of Jesus, told the people when they had no more wine. She said, **"Whatsoever he says to you, do it" (John2:5) NKJV.** When we develop this capacity to obey without questioning its rationale, we can have an uncommon boldness and confidence toward God. In the devotional book: *Faith to Faith*, Gloria Copeland asserts that "A life of obedience will give you a spiritual boldness you've never had before…a boldness in Prayer, a boldness in faith." This condition of Prayer is wholesomely expressed in I John 3:21-22:

> *"My dear friends, if we do not feel that we are doing wrong, we can be without fear when we come to God. And God gives us the things we ask for. We receive these things because we obey God's commands, and we do what pleases him" (ICB).*

ACTS OF SERVICE

One of the things that are pleasing to God is when we serve Him. It is through our service that we show that we genuinely love God. Service to God is one of the original ordinances of obedience. Deut 6:13 declares: **"You shall fear the Lord your God and serve Him,** and shall take oaths in His name." (NKJV). We see this command of obedience all through the lives of the patriarchs and even to the time when Jesus showed up in Galilee. During one of His bouts of temptation with the devil, the Lord Jesus responded by reemphasizing this act of serving God: **"Get behind Me, Satan! For it is written, 'You shall worship the Lord your God, and Him only you shall serve.'" (Luke 4:8, NKJV)**

Later on in His ministry, Jesus demonstrated that serving God is genuinely something with a great dividend (Exo23:25). Mark 10:45 concludes that: **Just as the Son of Man did not come to be served, but to serve, and to give His life a ransom for many." (NKJV).** Jesus went with the mentality of a servant even when He had the same equality as the God-head, yet He was willing to serve and subsequently was given a name that has authority over any other name (Phil 2:7-11). Service is a matter of choice, as Jesus explained in Luke 16:13, **"No servant can serve two masters; for either he will hate the one and love the other, or else he will be loyal to the one and despise the other. You cannot serve God and mammon." (NKJV).**

Equally, we see a similar admonishment from Joshua to the Israelites in Joshua 24:15: **"And if it seems evil to you to serve the Lord, choose for yourselves this day whom you will serve, whether the gods which your fathers served that *were* on the other side of the River or the gods of the Amorites, in whose land you dwell. But as for me and my house, we will serve the Lord." (NKJV).**

But someone might be thinking, are we not supposed to talk about prayer? Well, there are some intricacies involved. It is not just praying but getting a Yes to our prayer petition. We are looking at some things that could hinder getting that favorable answer and serving is one thing God does not take lightly.

The word serve is a derivative of the Latin meaning servant or slave. To put this in proper context, we can further elaborate on the definition of devotion. The word devotion (serve) would elicit such shades of meaning as being loyal, faithful, and committed to a person or a cause. So, to serve God is to be devoted, loyal, and committed to Him and the purpose of His kingdom agenda.

We see the strength of loyalty in organizations where some employees are more devoted than others. From the natural point of view, most bosses are always willing to go out of their way to do favors to those who are loyal and devoted to the organization. If that is understandable in the natural order of things and systems, why do we think it will be different from the spiritual order? The scripture says in Gal 6:7, **"Do not be deceived, God is not mocked; for whatever a man sows, that he will also reap." (NKJV)**

We see a classic example of getting a Yes to Prayer in the account of Cornelius in Acts 10: 1-2.

> *"There was a certain man in Caesarea called Cornelius, a centurion of what was called the Italian Regiment, a devout man and one who feared God with all his household, who gave alms generously to the people and prayed to God always." (NKJV).*

God had to reward Cornelius's loyalty with what he needed at the moment, which is to be filled with the Holy Spirit. God is always on the lookout for those that are devoted (Serve him) and be loyal to him. Take Apostle Paul, for instance, when he got into a shipwreck where all hope to be saved was lost, and everybody thought their life was over. They all needed a desperate divine intervention, but the only one they got came from a man that serves God. Later, Apostle Paul let them onto the secret of getting a Yes! in **Acts 27:23, "For there stood by me this night an angel of the God to whom I**

123

belong and whom I serve." (NKJV). Had these people not been found serving God, the story would have taken a different outcome.

I'm not saying that people go on a missionary journey to a remote place to prove their loyalty to God. We can always show our devotion to God in our little Jerusalem - our local assembly or church. We should be willing to carry out the assigned work or duty the leadership of such a meeting gives us. It could be to sing, clean, take care of kids, teach a class, handle the technical systems, parking, ushering, etc. The Lord always keeps the records.

There is this story told by Rev. Funke Adejumo about her sister not being able to conceive. She went to ask the Lord about this concern. God told her that the angels always bring the baby to church, but the sister is always found not available. Rev. Adejumo was confused because the sister is always in church for service, and yet the Lord is saying otherwise. At this point, God hinted that the angel brings the baby to the choir rehearsals on Saturdays, which is where the sister is supposed to be serving.

Well, apparently, after the sister got married and all that, she felt that singing in the choir was probably no big deal anymore. However, in the eyes of God, it is her place of devotion. So, she had to change her mindset and continued serving in the choir, and she got her answer to becoming a joyful mother. The scriptures say in Job 36:11, **"If they obey and serve *Him,* They shall spend their days in prosperity, And their years in pleasures." (NKJV)**

There are many things' people want to pray about, and their expectations are somewhat off the charts. As long as we are doing what pleases God through our obedience, there is an eternal assurance that God will fulfill His promise to us because He is a covenant-keeping God. He will keep his word just as He said in Exo 23:25: **So you shall serve the Lord your God, and He will bless your bread and your water. And I will take sickness away from the midst of you. (NKJV).**

UNSEEN RESOURCES - ANGELS

I believe the assurance that comes from God about getting a yes to prayers would not be complete without a brief on an important element of that agreement. We are talking about the ministry of Angels. Heb 1:14 let us understand that: **Are they not all ministering spirits sent forth to minister for those who will inherit salvation? (NKJV).**

Angels have been playing a significant role in the affairs of men since the beginning of time. Abraham (Gen 22:15), Jacob (Gen 32:1, Moses (Exodus 3:2), Joshua (Joshua 5:13-15), Gideon (Judges 6:12), David (I Chron 21:16), Elijah (1 Kings 19:5), Mary (Luke 1:26-30), Apostles (Acts 5:19), Peter (Acts 12:7-12), Paul (Acts 27:23), John (Rev 1:11, 22:8).

I remembered the first encounter I had with the ministry of an Angel over thirty years ago. I had just been cleared by my parents to be driving the family car, and I usually drop off my younger siblings in school. This particular morning, I had a commercial bus in front of me that I tried overtaking on a single lane road. I had swerved to the left to initiate the move, and I was halfway when I noticed another vehicle coming in my direction. Of course, I was not supposed to be there in the first place. I was far too gone to go back behind the commercial vehicle, and I had not completed the overtaking. I was just in-between, and my younger ones were just perplexed. It was as if I was losing my mind, and in that confusion, I temporarily took my hands off the steering wheel.

The next thing in a split-second, I saw the steering wheel turning left so that the oncoming vehicle could have the right of way and then instantly turn right back in my lane. It was like a movie, but I doubt if any stunt man would perform that kind of a feat. I must have lost consciousness for those brief seconds; the only thing I knew was the movie-like display. So, as I was getting the control back in my lane, I heard the Lord saying, **"Are they not all ministering spirits, sent forth to minister for them who shall be heirs of salvation? (KJV).** God was quoting that scripture to me in the King James version. After that, I was like, wow, I just got delivered by an angel. Since then, I've come to recognize their ministry and identify what I can gain from their service.

According to the estimate by Bishop Don Mears, there are more angels than humans, and there are about 20,000 angels assigned to every believer! Yes, angels are real even if we don't see them, but we have to take God at His word and believe what He says about them (2 Cor 4:18). Angels are a spiritual being with a specific duty to serve or wait on us. Can you imagine those big fellas waiting on us all day just waiting for a command from us?

There are two specific characteristics of Angels stated in **Ps 103:20: Bless the Lord, you His angels, Who excel in strength, who do His word, Heeding the voice of His word (NKJV).** The first thing we notice about angels is that they are very, very strong physically. Just one Angel in the Bible defeated 185,000 soldiers (Isa 37:36). The second thing we also observe that the Angels have an affinity towards the word of God. It seems they become activated by God's word. All through their encounter with people in the Bible, we see this theme in their actions.

We need to involve our angels in our daily living. They are waiting for our words and, more so, God's words on our lips. When I'm praying, I get them to assist in getting a yes by making specific demands. There is a classic one that kind of tops my relationship with my angels; it happened during my internship in the Eastern part of Nigeria. I stayed with my big sister and her family, and my immediate sister was supposed to visit us. She informed us in the morning as she was about boarding the bus. It was estimated to take about nine hours.

I got back from my work, and by 6 pm, she'd not arrived. Everyone was worried, and some of us went to the bus stop to become more concerned that something terrible might have happened. After everyone left the bus stop, I started pacing, and I was thinking about the angels that have been assigned to me according to Heb 1:14 and Ps 103:20. So, I started quoting those two scriptures to get me into the flow and put me in the position of a commander. Do you ever see soldiers on parade; they are always at attention, ready to obey the next instruction from their commanding officer.

Whenever you want to engage the angels assigned to you, you must have this Military posture picture in your mind. If you don't have it and are trying to be diplomatic, fearful, or uncertain about the outcomes you want, the angels would not respond. Of course, if they are on an assignment from God, as I shared in my first encounter with them, they will carry out that assignment with or without your input because they are getting their orders from another place.

What I'm talking about now is that when we want to put our angels to work, our minds will say so many things to us about it not being real, visible, etc. This is when we have to stick with what the Bible says and chunk whatever negative thoughts the mind might want to pop up.

I'm emphasizing this because this is the core of getting our angels to work. Faith-believe-word-assurance-confidence must all be on the line. There's no room for doubt, uncertainty, or let me just try it to see if it works, which is merely doubting. The attitude we need to have is similar to when someone says that you are not who you claim to be. We all know what we do when we are in that situation; we try to state our reasons and claims that we are exactly who we claim to be. That is the same thing at stake here.

There are a couple of elements involved when you want to command our Angels to work for us.

1. Assume the position of a military commander. (your word becomes a binding agreement).
2. State your delegated authority and right to command them (Heb 1:14, Ps 103:20).
3. Know the expected result you want (the Assignment).
4. State the expected result you want.
5. Overlay the scriptural references for this expected result.
6. Release, dispatch, and command them to get it done.

Anyway, as I was saying about my experience, once I got into the mood where I have a clear-cut idea of what I want; I started kind of recognizing the angels (You just have to believe that they are thereby your side), I declared what the Bible says about them and my authority to make a demand on them. I had a clear-cut goal in mind due to the lack of information about my sister's whereabouts. So, I said, "ministering Spirit, wherever my sister is right now, keep her safe from any harm, and ensure that she gets to us unharmed, I dispatch you now to go and bring her to us." I felt the burden of uncertainty lifted as I walked back to the house. I was not worried anymore because I'd committed her to the hand of the angel. At this point, heavens resources seemed to be the solution, and I agree with J. Edgar Hoover, who once said, "prayer is man's greatest means of tapping the infinite resources of God."

Some hours passed without any news, but at around 11 pm, we heard a knock at the gate. I went towards the gate, and there was a male voice asking to confirm my brother-in law's residence. I confirmed it. Then the Man introduced himself as a Police Inspector and that he has with him my sister, but he wanted to confirm the address before releasing her. He was acting as her protector.

The story was that the bus broke down along the way, so passengers were stranded on that road, and it was getting dangerously dark. Somehow the police came along and took everybody to their station for safety. After that, my sister was handed over to the Inspector to be delivered to her destination. The angel carried out the instructions I gave earlier. What you command, as long as it is promised in the scriptures, the angels are bound to obey and bring it to pass.

CHAPTER 6

COVENANT OF PRAYER

In our contemporary world of today, the term covenant might seem to be an archaic word. However, it does convey some standard terms we are familiar with. In this modern world of online presence and transactions, we are sometimes asked to sign certain agreement terms when making purchases, browsing a website (cookie download), and signing up for a membership. We see all these interactions as part of the norm of the 21st-century man or woman's everyday life experiences. In his classical model of *Transactional Analysis*, Dr. Eric Berne explained that interactions between individuals are similar to a call-and-response phenomenon. Since Prayer is an interactive dialogue between God and human beings, we can also apply the transactional analysis model to understanding the efficacy of prayers.

Prayer's covenant deals with established, acceptable, eternal terms of agreement, oath, contract, or engagement between God and humanity regarding the issue of prayers. There are numerous incidents in the Holy Scriptures where God talked about the terms of answering prayers. But first, we must understand that there is a difference between God hearing a prayer request versus God answering the prayer request.

Yes, God needs to listen to our pain, frustration, affliction, anguish, depression, and disappointments (Exo 3:7; Job 34:28;

Psalms 61:1; Psalms 102:20). King David understood this character of God hearing prayers when he said in **Psalms 65:2, "O You who hear prayer, To You all flesh will come" (NKJV)**. Again, he alluded to the importance of God hearing his prayers when he pleaded in Psalms 102:1, **"Hear my prayer, O Lord, And let my cry come to you" (NKJV)**

God is not just interested in hearing our prayers, but He also wants to answer them (Ps 20:1). It's no surprise then that God was very confident when He said in Jer 33:3, **"Call to Me, and I will answer you, and show you great and mighty things, which you do not know" (NKJV).**

God is always interested in giving us the desires of our hearts. He is a loving father who is looking out to fill our lives with moments of joy. The Bible says we should ask so that our satisfaction may be full (John 16:24). In the summer of 2018, my family moved to a bigger house with all the basic essential amenities I'd desired – double garage, finished basement, study, guest room, gym room, and spacious living room.

My brother and his family also needed to buy a bigger house than the one the family was living in. They had bided on quite a several houses, but someone was just always outbidding them at the end of the day because of the area they wanted with very competitive houses. The wife was getting tired, and her hope had started to dwindle. I'd been with them at open houses, and I could feel their heart.

One morning last summer, I started bringing their situation to God and telling Him about their desire to move to a bigger accommodation. I reminded God of their sacrifice in helping a family in a similar situation to purchase their house. Then I asked the Lord to give them a suitable, perfect house, just like mine.

On my way to work that morning, my brother called me to come to check on a house their agent sent him. As usual, they wanted to go check it out and wanted me to come along. We got to the house, and from the outside, it looked just like my house in terms of design, bricks, and color. I started making mental notes as we got into the house. It was perfect and had everything my brother and his wife wanted – a finished basement, deck, fence, study, a quiet neighborhood, and guest room. As expected, there had already been over 290 views on the house! So, they quickly put in their bid and didn't ask for any closing help. Their bid was selected, and they bought the house and moved into it, to the glory of God.

Throughout the Holy Bible's history, we see this peculiar God establishing himself with a solid reputation as a prayer-answering God. When God answers prayers, things happen, and the situation changes. The impossible becomes possible as dry bones become full human beings again (Eze 37). The dead are raised; joy and laughter replace sadness and grief. There is the reversal of life-threatening terminal cases, and lack gives way to supernatural abundance (I Kings 18:41)

THE PRAYER COVENANT

We see God establishing various covenants in the Bible. He made these covenants with individuals, groups of people, or nations. There was the Adamic (Gen 1:28-30); Noahic (Gen 9:8-17); Abrahamic (Gen 12:1-3, 17:2-7); Mosaic (Exo 19:1-6, 24:8, Deut 11:13-21); Davidic (2 Sam 7), Priestly (Num 18:19); and the New Birth Covenant (Jer 31:30-33).

We can view covenant from two dimensions. It could either be a conditional (obligatory) or a guaranteed (promissory) oath or agreement. In the obligatory covenant, there an element of uncertainty expressed by the words "if." Typically, conditional covenants are fulfilled if one of the parties does something, then the other party will then fulfill the terms of the agreement. Job 36: 11

shows that: **If they obey and serve *Him*, They shall spend their days in prosperity And their years in pleasures (NKJV).**

Conversely, the promissory covenant is borne with positive expectations from words such as "I will." In the scriptures, we see God making such a covenant to Abraham in Gen 17:1-2

> *"When Abram was ninety-nine years old, the Lord appeared to Abram and said to him, "I am Almighty God; walk before Me and be blameless. And I will make My covenant between Me and you, and will multiply you exceedingly" (NKJV).*

We see this covenant God made with Abraham being established by the seal of circumcision and later fulfilled when the Children of Israel left Egypt and dwelled in their land. God is the only one who gives the assurance of achieving a covenant. His unchanging character (Malachi 3:6) quickly makes him very dependable with his oaths and agreements.

THE SEAL OF APPROVAL

There is always a binding element between the two parties involved in every oath, contract, or agreement drafted. The signatories of the parties and any witnesses usually represent this element. This mandatory element is the potent seal that authorizes and enforces the actions of the parties involved. When it comes to answered prayers, the Sovereign God is the one who can initiate such a seal.

Some might wonder why the seal doesn't depend much on the other party – Man. The situation is because men, no matter how spiritual we are, will always have our humanity to contend with due to the fall of Man. As such, we observed people changing their minds about something they had initially agreed to fulfill. This propensity to change is unsuitable for a binding agreement that would likely have eternal consequences.

Consequently, it is heartwarming to hear God say in Psalm 89:34, **"My covenant I will not break, Nor alter the word that has gone out of My lips" (NKJV).**

After some four years of marriage, and my wife got pregnant, expecting our first child was a delightsome development. One evening, my wife told me she saw blood and thought we'd lost the pregnancy amid the excitement. When you hear such news, there is a tendency for our feelings and emotions to be overwhelmed by the reality of the events. I was about to wrap my head around what I had just heard when I got a nudging from the Holy Spirit reminding me of Ps 89:34. The scripture brought such immediate assurance, and I felt hopeful that nothing terrible would happen to the pregnancy. It was a very trying period because of the peculiar situation of the baby.

The doctors said fibroids were in my wife's womb, which might not allow the baby's development. The OBGYN specialists agreed with us to keep the baby and prescribed some strong medications to relieve the excruciating pain my wife was experiencing. My wife would often go into her pain mode, and we would pray, take the medicines, and then relief would come.

As the baby began to grow, the pain also increased, and more people from the church joined the prayer circle. After the prayers, my wife would dose off and sleep. This process seemed to be the routine until one night when all hell was let loose. The medications and the prayers seemed ineffective as my wife started wiggling in pain on the floor. She was on the verge of flushing the baby out because of the pain.

After I prayed the prayer of faith, I decided to keep a solemn mood to get a sense of direction from the Lord. As I was doing this, I was also making cursory glances at the TV screen because there was a Christian program at that time. Pastor Steve Munsey was ministering that day. Suddenly, he started saying there was a lady with a painful pregnancy and was in a dilemma about whether to keep the baby or flush the baby out due to the pain. Then he said, "God said He would give her relief tonight, and she will sleep like a baby, and the baby will be delivered." Praise the Lord! My wife slept like a log of wood that night as if she had taken sleeping medication. God is always faithful to His covenant promises.

The Prophet Balaam said concerning the reliability of God's means by announcing that:

> *"God is not a man, that He should lie, Nor a son of Man, that He should repent. Has He said, and will He not do? Or has He spoken, and will He not make it good? Num 23:19 (NKJV).*

In light of God's intrinsic nature, He has made an incredible spiritual agreement with His children concerning Prayer. This agreement gives us the assurance in the face of doubt or pestering unbelief that we can receive what we requested or asked for. Let's look at what God says concerning some of our prayer requests.

1. Jer 33:3 – **Call to Me, and I will answer you and show you great and mighty things, which you do not know (NKJV)**
2. Ps 2:8 – **Ask of Me, and I will give You The nations for Your inheritance, And the ends of the earth for Your possession (NKJV).**
3. Ps 50:15 – **Call upon Me in the day of trouble; I will deliver you, and you shall glorify Me (NKJV).**
4. Ps 91:15 – **He shall call upon Me, and I will answer him; I will be with him in trouble; I will deliver him and honor him (NKJV).**

5. Jer 29:12 – **Then you will call upon Me and go and pray to Me, and I will listen to you (NKJV).**
6. Mat 7:7-11 –
7. **"Ask, and it will be given to you; seek, and you will find; knock, and it will be opened to you. For everyone who asks receives, and he who seeks finds, and to him who knocks it will be opened. Or what man is there among you who, if his son asks for bread, will give him a stone? Or if he asks for a fish, will he give him a serpent? If you then, being evil, know how to give your children good gifts, how much more will your Father who is in heaven give good things to those who ask Him! (NKJV).**
8. Isa 41:17 – **"The poor and needy seek water, but there is none, Their tongues fail for thirst. I, the Lord, will hear them; I, the God of Israel, will not forsake them (NKJV).**
9. Isa 65:24 – **"It shall come to pass That before they call, I will answer; And while they are still speaking, I will hear (NKJV).**
10. Ps 65:2 – **O You who hear Prayer, To You all flesh will come (NKJV).**

We know from the ongoing discussion that there is Prayer, and there is also the covenant of Prayer, which deals with Prayer's expected outcome. When we engage in Prayer, we should realize the underlying contract of that Prayer as guaranteed by God. Prayer is a spiritual exercise where we link up with the power of God. Apostle Joshua Selman opined that "genuine prayer will transform you" The scripture in James 5:16 explained that:

> *"Therefore, confess your sins to one another [your false steps, your offenses], and pray for one another, that you may be healed and restored. The heartfelt and persistent prayer of a righteous man*

(believer) can accomplish much [when put into action and made effective by God—it is dynamic and can have tremendous power]. (AMP).

COVENANT RIGHT

We experience Prayer's power when the answer to that Prayer comes, and the request is granted. We might want to find an interesting question, "why is God obligated to answer prayer?" Can just about anybody pray and get God's attention? What if I had fallen into sin, disobedience, or unbelief? Will God still hear? We know from the scriptures that "**If I regard iniquity in my heart the Lord will not hear me (Ps 66:18, NKJV).**

First, we must understand that there are different types of prayers, and they all have different requirements. However, whether God will hear anyone due to sin or iniquity should not constitute this discussion's primary focus. There are some fundamental issues about why God answers prayers.

The pick of the pack for why God will readily answer a prayer is due to our creative rights. Every human on planet earth is linked to Adam, who is made in the image and God's likeness. This translates by common associative reasoning that we all have a creative right to God's image and likeness. We have the unique opportunity to approach God as our maker, irrespective of our state of sin or righteousness. Look at Cain in Genesis chapter 4, who murdered his brother Abel. Yes, it was documented that God was not pleased and even put a curse on him (Gen 4:11), yet Cain could have an audience and conversation with God. He later requested that God put a distinctive mark on him so that people won't be able to harm him and that God answered him (Gen 4:15).

There are sure consequences of sin and unrighteousness (Eze 18:4, Rom 6:23), sometimes leading to immediate judgment or a delayed punishment. These relationship dynamics are always at play in the daily relationship we have with our children. Yes, we love them, and there is nothing they would do that will make us disown them. We see these loving children misbehaving and getting into trouble, but now and then, we, as parents, are always there to apply the rule. There would be consequences for their actions, but at the same time, we are still eager to discuss with them and hear about their request. No wonder Jesus said in that Mat7:11, **"how much more shall your Father which is in heaven give good things to them that ask him" (KJV).**

For this underlying element, God will answer the very worst of sinners who turn to God in prayer. The scriptures declare that **"Whoever calls on the name of the Lord shall be saved" (Joel 2:32, Acts 2:21, Romans 10:13) NKJV.** So, if God hears us to be saved, He will also listen to us when we are afflicted, oppressed, confused, and going through any human trauma. The scripture says about God in Isa 49:16 **that "See, I have inscribed you on the palms of My hands; Your walls are continually before Me" (NKJV).**

The fact that we can turn to God in times of hardship, difficulty, and trauma shows that we trust His ability. This vestige of faith moves God to act and grant us the petition we request. We must remember that the patriarch Abraham displayed this kind of confidence before God that transformed him from an idol-worshiping person to be counted as a righteous friend of God (Gen 15:6).

We can contrast this phenomenon with what happened in the Garden of Eden when Adam and Eve didn't trust God. Their inability to believe what God said made them come under judgment and condemnation (Gen 3:12-19).

CHAPTER 7

CONFIDENCE IN PRAYER

Everything we have discussed so far is to give us an understanding of prayer and to imbue us with the possibilities that prayer affords everyone. Through prayer, God has made it abundantly possible for humanity to find complete solutions to myriad troubles and challenging situations. In the first chapter, we try to define and discuss what prayer is, and again, I want to capture the quintessence meaning of prayer:

1. Prayer is God's prescribed **antidote** for our troubles.

Is anyone among you in trouble? Let them pray. Is anyone happy? Let them sing songs of praise. James 5:13 (NIV)

2. Prayer is God's **solution center** for our problems, trials, and troubles.

Don't blame fate when things go wrong—trouble doesn't come from nowhere. It's human! Mortals are born and bred for trouble, as certainly as sparks fly upward. "If I were in your shoes, I'd go straight to God, I'd throw myself on the mercy of God. Job 5:6-8 (MSG)

3. Prayer is God's **instrument** of elevation.

Hear my cry, O God; Listen to my prayer. From the end of the earth I call to You, when my heart is overwhelmed and weak; Lead me to the rock that is higher than I [a rock that is too high to reach without Your help] Psalm 61:1-2(AMP)

4. Prayer is what **decodes** God's Mysteries.

'Call to Me, and I will answer you, and show you great and [a]mighty things, which you do not know.' Jeremiah 33:3 (NKJV)

5. Prayer is God's **point** of deliverance.

And it shall come to pass, that whosoever shall call on the name of the Lord shall be delivered. Joel 2:32 (KJV)

I will call upon the Lord, who is worthy to be praised: so shall I be saved from my enemies. Ps 18:3 (KJV)

6. Prayer is God's **fulcrum** for changing destinies.

Jabez prayed to the God of Israel: "Bless me, O bless me! Give me land, large tracts of land. And provide your personal protection— don't let evil hurt me." God gave him what he asked. 1 Chronicles 4:10 (MSG)

7. Prayer is God's **pathway** to honor.

When they call on me, I will answer; I will be with them in trouble. I will rescue and honor them. Psalm 91:15 (NLT)

8. Prayer is our **witness** before God in heaven

Another angel, who had a golden censer, came and stood at the altar. He was given much incense to offer, with the prayers of all God's people, on the golden altar in front of the throne. 4 The smoke of the incense, together with the prayers of God's people, went up before God from the angel's hand. Revelation 8:3-4 (NIV)

I believe the more we understand the true meaning of prayer, the better We develop a conscious mindset that assures us that God will hear and answer our prayers. The Scripture tells us in 1 John 5:14

"And this is the confidence that we have in him, that, if we ask anything according to his will, he heareth us." (KJV)

Grammy award winner CeCe Winans shares her first-hand testimony of unshakable faith and confidence in God. She was at the hospital with her family to see her brother being operated on at the theatre. The Doctors came out to meet the family, saying they had lost Ronald. Her father asked the Doctor if they could pray for him so he could go back and continue to work on Ronald. The family gathered and prayed and laid hands on the Doctor, who went back to give it another try. The next thing they knew, Ronald was resuscitated after successful surgery and later moved to the recovery room. Praise the Lord! Our prayers always produce answers.

If there is any acme point of answered prayer, it is the confidence and feeling of certainty. Apostle Paul even amid a shipwreck, dared to say in Acts 27:22-25

"And now I exhort you to be of good cheer: for there shall be no loss of any man's life among you, but of the ship. For there stood by me this night the angel of God, whose I am, and whom I serve, Saying, Fear not, Paul; thou must be brought before Caesar: and, lo, God hath given thee all them that sail with thee. Wherefore, sirs, be of good cheer: for I believe God, that it shall be even as it was told me." (KJV)

The Prophet Elijah displayed this level of confidence too when he challenged the 450 prophets of Baal in 1 Kings 18:36 – 38

"And it came to pass at the time of the offering of the evening sacrifice, that Elijah the Prophet came near, and said, Lord God of Abraham, Isaac, and of Israel, let it be known this day that thou art God in Israel, and that I am thy servant, and that I have done all these things at thy word.

Hear me, O Lord, hear me, that this people may know that thou art the Lord God, and that thou hast turned their heart back again.

Then the fire of the Lord fell, and consumed the burnt sacrifice, and the wood, and the stones, and the dust, and licked up the water that was in the trench." (NKJV)

Elijah was so confident that God would answer by fire that he dared the people to water the sacrifice three times. The natural mind will think that water should put out the fire, but then we understand that there are seven different kinds of fire extinguishers categorized according to the different types of fires, from the dry powder fire extinguisher, wet chemical, carbon monoxide, to dry chemical fire extinguisher. Not all fires can be extinguished by water. Elijah was so confident that God would answer, and He did.

In another vivid example in the Bible in John chapter 11, there was the case of Lazarus, who died, and we observed Jesus telling his disciples that though he was dead, He would wake him up. Where do we think Jesus garnered such audacity and assurance that Lazarus would be raised up from the dead?

"These things He said, and after that He said to them, "Our friend Lazarus sleeps, but I go that I may wake him up." John 11:11 (NKJV)

When Jesus got to the town, He met Lazarus' sisters and told them to believe and later asked the people to take away the stones to the tomb (John 11:41). Jesus' prayer was so full of confidence that is second to none:

"And Jesus lifted up His eyes and said, 'Father, I thank You that You have heard Me. And I know that You always hear Me, but because of the people who are standing by I said this, that they may believe that You sent Me.' Now when He had said these things, He cried with a loud voice, 'Lazarus, come forth!'

And he who had died came out bound hand and foot with graveclothes, and his face was wrapped with a cloth. Jesus said to them, Loose him, and let him go." (John 11:41-45) NKJV

When we go through the Bible, we see many men and women who dared to believe in God and demonstrated earth-shaking confidence. Natural behaviors seemed risky then, but the desired uncommon result happened at the end of the day. We see Father Abraham in Gen 24:7-10 giving assurance to his servant that the Lord will lead him to get a wife for his son Isaac.

We are still in awe of the audacity of the three Hebrew men, Shadrach, Meshach, and Abednego, who defied the pronouncements of the great King Nebuchadnezzar and refused to bow to a graven image (Daniel 3: 3-30). I always love their statement:

"Shadrach, Meshach, and Abednego, answered and said to the King, O Nebuchadnezzar, we are not careful to answer thee in this matter. If it be so, our God whom we serve is able to deliver us from the burning fiery furnace, and he will deliver us out of thine hand, O King. But if not, be it known unto thee, O King, that we will not serve thy gods, nor worship the golden image which thou hast set up." (Daniel 3:16-18, KJV)

Queen Esther was a woman of uncommon courage and had confidence that there would be a change in the situation of the Jews and dared to say: **"Go, gather all the Jews that are present in Susa, and observe a fast for me; do not eat or drink for three days, night or day. I and my maids also will fast in the same way. Then I will go in to [see] the King [without being summoned],**

which is against the law; and if I perish, I perish." (Esther 4:16. AMP)

The Prophet Elijah also demonstrated unusual confidence in God by locking up the rain over the land (I Kings 17, KJV). Equally, David, the shepherd boy, also projected unusual confidence in God when faced with the giant Goliath:

"Then said David to the Philistine, Thou comest to me with a sword, and with a spear, and with a shield: but I come to thee in the name of the Lord of hosts, the God of the armies of Israel, whom thou hast defied. This day will the Lord deliver thee into mine hand; and I will smite thee, and take thine head from thee; and I will give the carcasses of the host of the Philistines this day unto the fowls of the air, and to the wild beasts of the earth; that all the earth may know that there is a God in Israel." (I Samuel 17:45-46. KJV)

CONFIDENCE IS A REFLECTION OF KNOWLEDGE

For anyone to put confidence in another person, there must have been an initial interaction between them. We usually don't just trust or believe someone we do not know or have not met. We can't just do it. Therefore, our trust in God is based on interaction, relationship, and conviction through knowledge. There are three essential commodities of God's knowledge: Experiential knowledge, Progressive knowledge, and Revelational knowledge. I see them as commodities that indicate their significance as tangible assets that can be acquired, developed, and increased in value.

EXPERIENTIAL KNOWLEDGE – the holy scriptures have shown numerous times that we can only know God when we experience Him. This assertion is summed up in **Dan 11:32b "but the people that do know their God shall be strong and do exploits" (KJV)**. In the Holy Bible, such knowledge might involve supernatural encounters (Exodus 3:1-4), divine instructions (Gen 12:1), dreams & vision (Gen 46:2; Numbers 24:15-16), miracles & healings (John 2:11), and various expressions of Godhead through the ministry of the Holy Spirit as I mentioned in the chapter.

We cannot attempt to know a God that is a Spirit with our natural senses; we would need a spiritual modulator to be at His level (I Cor 2:9-12). While talking about the courage to stand up to the devil, Kenneth Copeland said, "that kind of confidence only comes from personal knowledge of God through time spent in prayer and fellowship with Him." It is such unnatural knowledge of God that imbue men and women to act as if they are crazy in the face of challenges or difficulties.

This experiential knowledge gives the needed spiritual energy or strength. The experiential knowledge is what assured David to confront Goliath. It formed the bedrock of Shadrach, Meshach, and Abednego's defiance of the King's command. They all knew God more practically and not just in theory.

PROGRESSIVE KNOWLEDGE – after we have an experiential knowledge of God, it will naturally lead us to the second rung of knowing God – the pursuit of more of God's presence. **Hosea 6:3 says**

"Then shall we know, if we follow on to know the Lord: his going forth is prepared as the morning; and he shall come unto us as the rain, as the latter and former rain unto the earth".(KJV).

Yes, we may have had a practical knowledge of God, but that is not the complete knowledge of God. There was a time when the Israelites faced the Syrian army, and they said, based on a past encounter with the God of Israel, that He is only the God of the hills and not the valleys. However, on the seventh day, the Lord showed them that He is both the God of the valleys and the hills, and 100 thousand Syrian armies were killed **(1 Kings 20:26-29).** There are many ways He can answer our prayers; we must learn to flow with what He's saying (Rhema). The trumpeter and songwriter Nathaniel Bassey shared a marvelous testimony of a woman who attended one of his praise concerts. He said that during the praise sessions, he sensed the anointing and heard himself telling the people that they shouldn't pray but sing when they get home and there's a problem.

A woman in Festac Town, Nigeria got home after the concert and met people crying, and she was curious as to what was happening, only to be informed that her 15-year daughter had died and was on the way to the mortuary. She remembered the instruction and started to sing to the confusion of everybody who expected a different reaction from her. After a while, the girl on the way to the mortuary sneezed and got up from the death bed. Hallelujah!

God is all-knowing, but we only know in part. He reveals more of Himself a little here, a little there (Isa 28:10). Apostle Paul had a burning desire for this kind of knowledge when he declared, **"That I may know him, and the power of his resurrection, and the fellowship of his sufferings, being made conformable unto his death" (Philippians 3:10, KJV)**. Likewise, Apostle Peter also recommended that **"But grow in grace, and in the knowledge of our Lord and Saviour Jesus Christ. To him be glory both now and forever. Amen." (2 Peter 3:18)**

REVELATIONAL KNOWLEDGE – the first and second commodity of God's knowledge deals with "I know God because I have encountered Him, and I am increasing in that knowledge."

These two are seen as a graduated path of knowledge. However, there is a kind of God's knowledge that comes in an unexpected, multidimensional way devoid of human involvement. (Galatians 1:12 KJV). This knowledge represents an unveiling or revealing of mystery (Ephesians 3:3). The main feature of God's revelational knowledge is that it makes you act per what has been revealed

(Galatians 2:2). It has the power and ability to make you agree with the word, instruction, or dream.

CONFIDENCE IS AN ACT OF OUR FAITH.

A lot is being shared about faith, and faith is not an abstract of some religious creed. Faith is the tangible element of the supernatural and is always based on a supernatural knowledge of God. The Scripture gives us a pathway in Romans 10:13-17

"For whosoever shall call upon the name of the Lord shall be saved. How then shall they call on him in whom they have not believed? and how shall they believe in him of whom they have not heard? and how shall they hear without a preacher?

And how shall they preach, except they be sent? as it is written, How beautiful are the feet of them that preach the gospel of peace, and bring glad tidings of good things!

But they have not all obeyed the gospel. For Esaias saith, Lord, who hath believed our report? So then faith cometh by hearing, and hearing by the word of God" (KJV)

Just as the natural man receives information through our five senses to act, we also need our faith sense to take supernatural actions. Every natural or supernatural effort is always based on information or knowledge. Jesus told the people to "take away the stone" because he had information that God had heard His prayers. In like manner, Elijah told the people to pour water on the sacrifice three times. He knew something they didn't know.

I remember seeking a place for my internship during my fourth year in an Engineering course in college. I applied to the Shell Petroleum, Port Harcourt Nigeria but was told that the current batch of interns needs to complete their before I can be absorbed. That would mean spending four months doing nothing, so I went with my friend to knock on the doors of companies willing to take in an intern.

We got to the communication center, where Shell Petroleum had numerous communications contractors. I walked to the office of PPC, a Shell Petroleum contractor, and met the boss, who told me they needed a Youth Copper (A college graduate), not someone still in school. However, I developed an interest in telecoms and believe it is the right fit.

The boss sent my aptitude test to the HQ, but I was still determining if they would take me since I needed to qualify. As God would allow it, the manager called me and said headquarter office wanted me on board, and I was accepted. Praise God! Our assurances always give us a quiet inner peace that says, "I know how it will turn out in the end."

CONFIDENCE GROWS WITH JURISDICTION

I believe that God wants us to have an unshakable trust in His ability to answer all our prayers and get the answers we so desperately need. However, as we have discussed in earlier chapters, there are some fundamental elements to getting these answers to prayers. As we conclude this book, I want to make an impression about having the confidence to get a yes to prayers.

There is a myth I think we need to get rid of, and that is the limit some people put on the time God will or can answer prayers. Some people believe that God only answers some prayers at midnight or during a particular hour of the day. Yes, God might have expressed himself to such individuals during those time frames (Experiential Knowledge), but He is not limited to those times.

Let us remember that God created time: "**And God said, Let there be lights in the firmament of the heaven to divide the day** from the night; and let them be for signs, and for seasons, and for days, and years." **(Gen 1:14. KJV).** Also, Ps 104:19 declares that "**He appointed the moon for seasons: the sun knoweth his going down**" **(KJV).**

Furthermore, He is also the one who can change the times and seasons (Dan 2:21). We then can conclude that God is not time bound and is not controlled by time. Therefore, our prayers are not meant to be limited by location, locality, time, or season. So, we can pray anytime and anywhere according to these scriptural insights:

"Now Jesus was telling the disciples a parable to make the point that at all times they ought to pray and not give up and lose heart." (Luke 18:1)(AMP)

"I desire therefore that in every place men should pray, without anger or quarreling or resentment or doubt [in their minds], lifting up holy hands." (1 Timothy 2:8) AMPC

It is essential to understand that:

MEN CAN PRAY EVERYWHERE
BECAUSE GOD IS EVERYWHERE

This issue of praying everywhere and anytime brings us to the concluding discussion on jurisdiction. The dictionary gives us an excellent description of the word.

Jurisdiction is the official power to make legal decisions and judgments.

When we begin to peel off the various shades of meaning of jurisdiction, we come to some exciting connotations:

1. Recognized power, right, and ability to make legal decisions and judgments.

2.   Authority or privilege to make decisions or judgments.

Understanding the mega role jurisdiction plays in developing confidence in prayers is necessary. When people relocate from outside the U.S. or from other states to Maryland, they usually need a driver's license issued by the State of Maryland. They might even have a teenager turning 17 years old, and he would need a new license. So, for whatever reason, he must process a new driver's license to enable him to drive a vehicle in the State of Maryland, even when such an individual already has an out-of-state license.

The old permit must be turned in to the MVA for a Maryland license. It is all about jurisdiction. We would need an official authority (A driver's license) to drive on a Maryland road. When I get on the I-95 highway, I'm full of confidence that I have the legal right to be on that road without any fear of cops pulling me over. Our confidence is always boosted by the legal authority backing us.

In the law enforcement terrain, a New York Police officer cannot travel to Colorado to arrest a criminal. Even though he has the case file of the criminal for years, the badge on him is that of the state of New York, and he has crossed state boundaries. When in Colorado, he is out of range or outside of his sphere of authority (jurisdiction).

The Police officer has two options if he wants to arrest the criminal. He can either wait until the person of interest comes back to New York or collaborate with other local law enforcement agents in Colorado. He can equally turn his case over to other federal agencies, such as the FBI, with jurisdiction across the 50 states.

ELEMENTS OF JURISDICTION

As I stated in the earlier chapter, prayer is a unique platform that allows us to invite and authorize God to perform and work out things for us on earth. We also need to recognize that prayers give us so much ability to wield authority. God wants us to pray every kind or type of prayer.

"With all prayer and petition pray [with specific requests] at all times [on every occasion and in every season] in the Spirit, and with this in view, stay alert with all perseverance and petition [interceding in prayer] for all [e] God's people" (Ephesians 6:18) (AMP)

This divine expectation of praying everywhere and at any time of the day is one of the confidence boosters essential to answered prayers.

RHEMA WORD

There are two other essential elements of the jurisdiction of prayer upon which our confidence grows. The first is the word of God and the second is the Holy Spirit. We see in **Psalm 119:89**

"Forever, O Lord, Your word is settled in heaven [standing firm and unchangeable]." (AMP).

We can boldly say that, by default, there is divine jurisdiction anywhere the word of God is.

I was preparing to minister at a prayer retreat last year with the theme: Open Heavens. At times we can see heaven as something that requires much human effort to open. Still, the Lord ministered to me and said, "There will always be an open heaven whenever there is a Rhema word from God" I have already explained the different kinds of the word of God. The Rhema word always makes all the resources of heaven available because when God speaks, nothing can stop or hinder its manifestation. The preacher says in **Ecclesiastes 8:4, "Where the word of a king is, there is power; And who may say to him, "What are you doing?" (NKJV)**

No matter how the situation looks, what God says during your interaction with Him matters. That will give you the confidence that there will be a change in your circumstances. Apostle Paul was in a terrible shipwreck, and there were fears of losing human lives, yet God gave him a word that assured him. He was not dismayed and told the people, **"So keep up your courage, men, for I believe God and have complete confidence in Him that it will turn out exactly as I have been told." (Acts 27:25. AMP).** Anything God tells you; you can take to the bank and cash it. The Rhema word will always produce what was spoken per Isa 55:11

"So will My word be which goes out of My mouth; It will not return to Me void (useless, without result), Without accomplishing what I desire, And without succeeding in the matter for which I sent it." (AMP).

God's spoken word provides our jurisdiction for the answer we so desperately need. Our confidence invariably depends on the word we receive from God because He is only committed to whatever He has said. This commitment characterized the manner God gave Sarah a son in her old age. **"The Lord visited Sarah as He had said, and the Lord did for her as He had promised"** (Gen 21:1). Sometimes, the word can also be in the form of a prophecy like the numerous ones that spoke about the coming messiah – Jesus Christ.

"Therefore the Lord himself will give you a sign: The virgin will conceive and give birth to a son, and will call him Immanuel" (Isaiah 7:14)(KJV).

"When you ascended on high, you took many captives; you received gifts from people, even from the rebellious—that you, Lord God, might dwell there" (Psalm 68:18)(NIV)

The prophetic word can also be for a group of people, a family, or a nation. Of particular interest in our contemporary time is the word of prophecy given by the British Missionary Pa Sydney Elton in 1986 about the nation of Nigeria: *"Nigeria and Nigerians will be known all over the world for corruption. Your name – Nigeria will stink for corruption but after a while, a new phase will come – a phase of righteousness. People from the nations of the earth will hold a Nigerian and say," We want to follow you to your nation to go and learn righteousness.'*

The word of prophecy would still need to be accepted and prayed, and I will talk more about this in my other forthcoming book: *Depth of Conviction: Politics and the Divine Mandate,* due spring next year. For now, let's conclude this discussion on confidence in prayers.

HOLY SPIRIT INFLUENCE

We have come to the conjunction of the second element of jurisdiction of prayer, which is the impact and influence of the Holy Spirit. The Prophet Isaiah captures these two essential elements in **Isaiah 34:16 "Seek out of the book of the Lord and read: not one of these [details of prophecy] shall fail, none shall want and lack her mate [in fulfillment]. For the mouth [of the Lord] has commanded, and His Spirit has gathered them." (AMP). "The Holy Spirit is the eternal power that backs up the word of God." (John 6:63)**

The presence of the Holy Spirit gives us the spiritual latitude, authority, and boldness that we are asking will be granted. We need to be conscious of the Holy Spirit to increase our confidence that our prayers will get a yes. Then we can conclude like Apostle Paul that **"And we know that all things work together for good to them that love God, to them who are the called according to his purpose." (Roman 8:28) (KJV)**

The ability to speak in tongues or to pray in the Holy Ghost helps to build up spiritual power or energy (Jude:20). Have you ever started praying in tongues for anything, and yet your understanding is blank? Your mind does not have the faintest idea of what you are praying for; all you know is that you are praying in tongues. Then when you are done praying, it seems something is still missing. It seems you didn't grab the answer and leave that place of prayer without the confidence that God will do it. All you got was hope that something would happen but with no specifics.

Speaking in tongues is a spiritual ability given to our newborn again spirit man, which is different from the Holy Spirit. Speaking in tongues does not mean I have engaged the Holy Spirit in my prayers. It simply means my spirit man is talking. In chapter two, about the Centrality of the Holy Spirit, I mentioned the concept of Holy Spirit-initiated prayers.

Now let's conclude with the four processes of how the Holy Spirit helps our confidence to know that what we pray for is coming or it's done.

1. There is a burden about the answer – having a desire or burden for something is necessary. Without a burden, a wish, or an expectation, the Holy Spirit is jobless.

   In Gen 1:2, we see the first mention of the Holy Spirit here and the relationship between a need, burden, desire, expectations, and Holy Spirit activity: The earth was without form, and an empty waste and darkness was upon the face of the very great deep. The Spirit of God was moving (hovering, brooding) over the face of the waters. (AMP). The Holy Spirit is mandated to birth things for us in the supernatural realm (1 Cor 2:9-10).

2. There was a pick-up from stores – during the surge of the COVID-19 pandemic. Most stores established a pick-up policy for customers, where you order online and go through a drive-through to pick up what you ordered. The Holy Spirit is the one who helps us to pick up our prayer orders. The things God gives us are usually beyond human comprehension. **1 Cor 2:9-10 shows "But, on the contrary, as the Scripture says, What eye has not seen and ear has not heard and has not entered into**

the heart of man, [all that] God has prepared (made and keeps ready) for those who love Him [[a]who hold Him in affectionate reverence, promptly obeying Him and gratefully recognizing the benefits He has bestowed]. Yet to us God has unveiled and revealed them by and through His Spirit, for the [Holy] Spirit searches diligently, exploring and examining everything, even sounding the profound and bottomless things of God [the [b]divine counsels and things hidden and beyond man's scrutiny]." (AMP)

So, even though I am praying in tongues, I cannot pick up things from God if I am unaware of the content. This gap is the infirmity the Holy Spirit helps us with, as highlighted in Roman 8:26. During the store pick-up, we are requested to present an Identification such as a driver's license. It is the same with God, who always demands to know what's in the mind of the Holy Spirit (Rom 8:27)

I know someone would think that God will not hear me if I am not filled with the Holy Ghost. The answer is no. God answers prayers whether you are filled with the Holy Spirit or not. We are here to see how we can establish better assurances to get better answers. It's like the superlative's narrative of good-better-best. There are good answers, better answers, and the best answers.

3. There is a witness – after a burden (Rom 8:26) and subsequent collection (Isa 34:16, Rom 8:27), the Holy Spirit will send the spirit man a confirming receipt known as an inner witness. This witness gives us that needed confidence when we get up from the place of prayer that God has done it. It gives us that stoic attitude that we know, and it's as real to us as our names. This certainty is like when we receive the gift of salvation through Jesus Christ, an operation of the Holy Spirit.

The Lord wants us to have confidence in our prayers when we engage the same principles that worked when we got saved. The more we engage the Holy Spirit before even speaking in tongues, the more He will help our natural limitations and gather the answers and solutions for us with confirmatory Yes!

FINAL WORDS

One of the essential points of this book is to illustrate that God can and is always eager to hear us when we pray, and He is still delighted to grant us our heart's desires. I have described the fundamental pillars of getting our prayers heard and the importance of the Holy Spirit's ministry. We considered the assurance from understanding God's will concerning our desires.

We have looked at the underlay of the answered prayer process as expounded by Jesus Christ Himself in the needed connectivity and the conditionalities attached to this process. We equally got a glimpse of the covenant God made and established concerning answering the prayer of every man and woman on planet earth. All these truths develop unshakable confidence in our prayer life.

In this book's beginning chapters, I mentioned that some more in-depth Prayer substances were deliberately left out. However, most of this addenda will be compiled in the sequel edition of the book. It is essential always to get the right foundation for anything we want to show or explain before moving to the more complex stuff. Thank you for giving me the audience to read through, and the knowledge and insight gained would, in no small way, lead to more of our prayers being answered in Jesus's Name.

Dr. F. Allan Olorunsola.
Maryland, USA.

ENDNOTES

Chapter 1:
Connotations of Prayer

[1] Meriam-Webster Online Dictionary copyright © 2005 by Meriam-Webster, Incorporated, **s.v.** "Prayer"
[2] Meriam-Webster Online Dictionary copyright © 2005 by Meriam-Webster, Incorporated, **s.v.** "Pray"

Chapter 3:
Concerning The Will of God

[1] Vine's Expository Dictionary of Old and New Testament Words © 1996 by Thomas Nelson Inc, Publishers, s.v. "Understand"

PRAYER OF SALVATION

The primary reason Jesus Christ came to the world is to save men and women (Matthew 1:21). He brought the lost eternity within our reach. All we have to do is accept the free gift of eternal life according to John 3:16 *"For God so loved the world that He gave His only begotten Son, that whoever believes in Him should not perish but have everlasting life."* Just like everything God has given humanity, we still need to pray to receive them.

Are you ready to accept God's Son, Jesus Christ, into your life? Then let us approach God based on his word in Romans 10:9-10 *"that if you confess with your mouth the Lord Jesus and believe in your heart that God has raised Him from the dead, you will be saved. For with the heart one believes unto righteousness, and with the mouth confession is made unto salvation."*

If you will accept Jesus Christ as your Lord and Savior, please pray this prayer out aloud and mean it with all your heart:

Dear Heavenly Father, I acknowledge that I am a sinner, and I ask you to forgive me of my sins. I believe Jesus Christ died for my sins and rose again to make me righteous. I now invite Jesus Christ to come into my heart as my savior and become the Lord of my life. I am willing to follow and obey Christ, and I ask you to fill me up with your Holy Spirit. Thank you for saving me and making me the righteousness in God (2Cor 5:21).

**If you have received Jesus Christ as your savior,
please feel free to contact us at *info@selahskript.com***

ABOUT THE AUTHOR

Dr. Allan Olorunsola is an ordained minister and kingdom practitioner. His many years of an intimate walk with the Lord have made him understand many kingdom mysteries about prayers and the unraveling of God's will as it pertains to divine purpose. He has been part of many prayer campaign platforms and groups. He is the coordinating minister of Rhema Chapel International Churches in the North America region.

When not ministering, Dr. Olorunsola has been a creative entrepreneur, licensed Youth Soccer coach, and President of the Global Impact Sports Soccer Academy. An Engineer in IT and Telecommunication over the past two decades. He has a few master's degrees and a Doctorate in Computer Science. He is married, blessed with children, and lives in the Washington Metro Area.

Author contact: allan.olorunsola@gmail.com

Selah Skript Publishing
P. O. Box 2568. Silver Spring, MD 20915
www.selahskript.com